PREPARING STUDENTS TO RAISE ACHIEVEMENT SCORES

Grades 7–8

by Darriel Ledbetter and
Leland Graham

Incentive Publications, Inc.
Nashville, Tennessee

The authors gratefully acknowledge
the assistance and suggestions of the following persons:

Virginia Brickman, Stan Carey, Harriett Cook, Darwin Felion,
Chris Higgins, Sue Kennedy, Martha Lee, Frankie Long,
Isabelle McCoy, Beverly Moody, Jennifer Moore, Melanie Moore,
Dan Payne, Pat Slaton, John Spilane, and Nancy Zwald.

Illustrated by Kathleen Bullock
Cover by Marta Drayton and Joe Shibley

ISBN 0-86530-341-X

PRINTED IN THE UNITED STATES OF AMERICA

Table of Contents

INTRODUCTION

It has become increasingly important that students be trained to improve the skills that allow them to succeed when taking standardized tests. National average achievement standards are being developed for all ages and for all academic areas. The best classes, schools, and futures will belong to those students who develop the best test-taking skills.

There are many different types of achievement tests. Students should learn a variety of strategies and skills so that their true knowledge is reflected in all achievement scores. Test-taking skills in this book include those in the following areas:

reading comprehension;

vocabulary and spelling;

math concepts and computations;

language mechanics;

interpreting maps, charts, and diagrams; and

use of the library.

Parents and teachers who help students learn to make use of the test-taking strategies and skills in this book will invariably see students' achievement scores improve. An improvement in achievement scores means positive reinforcement of a student's self-confidence, resulting in improved performance in all areas of academic work.

CHAPTER ONE:

MASTERING STUDY TECHNIQUES AND TEST-TAKING SKILLS

In this chapter you will find the basic techniques that will help you study more effectively and improve your test scores. In order to make the best use of these skills, follow these helpful study hints:

- **Find a proper study area in which to work.**
  The best place would be a quiet, well-lit study area away from family interruptions, distractions, and conversations.

- **Designate a regular study time or period.**
  Set aside time each day to study. During this designated time, all other activities should cease: no phone calls, no television, no friends' visits, and no interruptions from parents or other family members.

- **Keep a daily, weekly, or monthly planner.**
  Keeping a planner (see following pages) is a good way to keep track of all of your assignments, upcoming tests, after-school activities, family outings, and household chores. The left column of the daily planner is for listing assignments for various periods. The right column will help you plan your day as well as schedule appointments and events. Make a copy of the daily assignment planner and list your current subjects in order. Then make enough copies of this master planning page to serve your needs.

- **Obtain all the proper materials for your study area.**
  Be sure to have all the proper school supplies that you need in order to study. Your study area should include: pencils, colored pencils, pens, pencil sharpener, erasers, three-hole lined paper, three-ring binder, ruler, highlighter, paper clips, glue stick, index cards, student planner (daily, weekly, or monthly), dictionary, and thesaurus. If you have a home computer, it should be in your study area.

DAILY ASSIGNMENT PLANNER

ASSIGNMENTS

DATE _____

FIRST PERIOD _____

SECOND PERIOD _____

THIRD PERIOD _____

FOURTH PERIOD _____

FIFTH PERIOD _____

SIXTH PERIOD _____

8:00 A.M.
9:00 A.M.
10:00 A.M
11:00 A.M.
12:00 P.M.
1:00 P.M.
2:00 P.M.
3:00 P.M.
4:00 P.M.
5:00 P.M.
6:00 P.M.
7:00 P.M.

WEEKLY PLANNER

M	Tu	W

Th	F	Sa/Su

MONTH OF

SUNDAY	MONDAY	TUESDAY	WEDNESDAY	THURSDAY	FRIDAY	SATURDAY

MASTERING STUDY TECHNIQUES AND TEST-TAKING SKILLS

Perhaps one of the most useful study skills (tools) you will learn is note taking. You may think note taking is just for high school or college students, but this is a study skill you should develop as early as the middle grades. If you become a good note taker, you will do better on tests and written reports.

NOTEWORTHY TIPS . . .

- Come to class with necessary materials to take notes (for example, pencils are already sharpened).

- Pay close attention to your teacher and concentrate on what is being said.

- As you take notes, jot down important facts and ideas.

- Write the information in key words, phrases, clauses, or simple sentences. Do not be overly concerned about grammar or spelling while taking notes.

- Jot down any details, dates, and examples, for this is the type of information that is often asked on quizzes or tests. (Don't try to take word for word notes. Instead, listen to get the main idea.)

- Whenever possible, use abbreviations and symbols (for example, Jan = January; Sun = Sunday; AL = Alabama; ans = answer; ft = foot; % = percent).

- Begin to develop your own speed-writing or shorthand system. An easy method is by omitting vowels. Much time can be saved by using symbols instead of whole words when you are taking notes (for example, notebook = ntbk; report = rpt; project = prjct; and = &; at = @; directions = dir).

- Learn to ask questions when you do not understand what your teacher means.

- Reread your notes before leaving class to eliminate any confusion you may have.

PRACTICE TAKING NOTES

ACTIVITY: Your parent or teacher will read the following paragraphs aloud to you. On a sheet of notebook paper, take notes on the paragraphs as they are read, using speed-writing symbols, phrases, or clauses. When completed, compare your notes to the paragraphs as written.

Snakes are in the reptile family and are closely related to lizards. They are covered with small scales which are overlapping. They have movable eyelids and external ear openings. Their tongues are used for smell. The smallest snake is 8–12 inches long, and the largest measures about 8 feet.

From *Effective Language Arts Techniques for Middle Grades,* Incentive Publications. Used by permission.

Although the Africans call them goobers and the Spaniards call them cacahuate, we simply call them peanuts in the United States. Mediterranean adventurers originally brought peanuts back from their travels to Peru and began to raise their crops. Eventually Spanish and Portuguese explorers traded these crunchy treats with nearby Africa in exchange for spices and ivory.

From *180 Days Around the World,* Incentive Publications. Used by permission.

The Bermuda Triangle, which has received much attention in the past few years, has been the subject of many books, magazine articles, and radio and television talk shows. A television special was devoted to the Bermuda Triangle. Also, the Triangle figures in the UFO and ancient astronaut mysteries. According to all accounts, there is something very strange occurring out there.

In this particularly stormy and changeable patch of ocean called the Bermuda Triangle, ship and plane losses can be sudden, surprising, and fatal. Frequently, there are no calls for help, no survivors, no bodies, and no wreckage. A ship may sail into a calm sea under a cloudless sky—then vanish. A plane may disappear there after reporting that "all is well." Some people that have supposedly disappeared in the Triangle have been captured by countries such as Cuba.

Commercial and military craft cross this area safely every day. Since 1954, more than fifty ships and aircraft have vanished in or near the Bermuda Triangle. Of the alleged ships and planes lost mysteriously during the last 100 years, most have met misfortune in the months of December and January.

From *How to Write a Great Research Paper,* Incentive Publications. Used by Permission.

Now that you have practiced note taking, the next step is to read your notes aloud. You and a classmate or family member should read your notes to each other. Also, please keep in mind that the notes written quickly in class can sometimes be difficult to read and understand. In these cases, while the information is still fresh in your mind, **rewrite** your notes so that you can understand what you have written. You can strengthen or **reinforce** your notes by adding important information from your textbook. Then use a highlighter to **spotlight** important facts, dates, and names in your notes.

In order to remember names, dates, facts, and other information from your notes, develop your own mnemonic devices. A memory device, often written in the right-hand margin, can be a word, phrase, or even a picture. Whatever device you create will help you recall the information while studying or taking a test.

GENERAL NOTES   ABBREVIATIONS   MNEMONIC DEVICE

Memory Device

Notes

Notes	Memory Device
Wm. Shakespeare, Eng. playwright; born 1564; died 1616; from mdle class family; left fam. at 20 to pursue playwriting career; opend Globe thea. in 1599	1564 / 1616 / 20 / Globe
U.S., fifty states; "mltg pot" of many peoples; cap: Washington, DC, main lang: English; AK, lgst. st; VA, home lgst. no. pres.	US / DC / AK / VA
Stand in 4 states at same time: Arizona, New Mexico, Colorado & Utah	UT | CO / AZ | NM

Studying for a test involves many skills. If you have completed all your class and homework assignments, listened carefully, and taken thorough notes, you should be ready for your test review time. The more you study for your test, the more confidence you will naturally have. Here are some helpful hints in the final preparation for taking any test:

- **Do not spend precious study time** reviewing information you already know.

- If possible, **create your own flash cards** (index cards with questions written on one side and answers written on the other). These cards are useful for learning the most difficult of concepts.

- **Review** your class notes and homework assignments as needed.

  If necessary, use your mnemonic device for an additional review. Again, flash cards may be helpful if you are having difficulty remembering the information.

- Next, **study** your textbook notes and follow the same procedures as mentioned for your class notes.

- **Create** information time lines, charts, and/or tables wherever appropriate.

- Finally, give yourself a **five-minute quick review** before a test for any area(s) that may cause concern.

How to successfully take tests: The test papers are handed out and the teacher has announced "Begin!" What should you do next? Take a few minutes or so to . . .

- **Before you begin the test,** take a few deep breaths in order to calm yourself.

- **Read all the directions carefully.** (Errors are made because students misread the directions for test questions.)

- **Pay attention to the directions at the bottom of the pages.** Sometimes you are instructed to **GO ON** to the next page and other times to **STOP!**

- **Skim the entire test as quickly as possible.**

- **Use your "memory device"** if necessary to jot down a word or a picture on the back of a page to jog your memory for later.

- **Do not spend too much time on one problem or question.** Move on, and if you have time, come back to it.

- **If you find yourself becoming confused** or even drawing a blank, stop, stare into space, try to clear your mind, take a few deep breaths, and then resume the test.

- **If you finish your test early,** and if it is permitted, go back and check your work on any unsure or flagged question(s).

- **Remember, first thoughts are generally correct.** Do not make the mistake of second-guessing yourself.

- **If you need to change an answer,** be sure to erase your original answer completely.

- **The best advice:** Be rested and alert the day of testing.

CHAPTER TWO:

IMPROVING VOCABULARY SKILLS

In the first chapter, you learned various study techniques and test-taking skills. The purpose of this chapter is to improve your vocabulary skills by looking at various strategies to help you understand word usage. These strategies include: sound, structure, context clues, and a dictionary. With a greater understanding of words and how they are used, your own vocabulary achievement scores will naturally improve.

ACTIVITY: For each question below, decide which one of the four answers is closest in meaning to the word in bold type above it. Fill in the bubble for the word that is closest in meaning.

 *Think about the meaning of the word (not the part of speech) in **bold type** before you select an answer.*

1. To **retrieve** the money
   - ○ get back
   - ○ borrow
   - ○ lose
   - ○ pay back

2. He finished his **thesis.**
   - ○ a musical play
   - ○ a main idea
   - ○ a short novel
   - ○ a fourteen-line poem

3. A **cantankerous** old man
   - ○ easy going
   - ○ friendly
   - ○ talkative
   - ○ bad-tempered

4. To **fluctuate** the prices
   - ○ remain unchanged
   - ○ kept high
   - ○ go up and down
   - ○ rise constantly

STOP

WORDS AND THEIR MEANINGS

ACTIVITY: For each question, you are to decide which of the four answers is closest in meaning to the word in **bold type** above it. Circle the correct answer.

1. A feeling of **gratitude**
   A uncertainty
   B thankfulness
   C excitement
   D anger

2. An **arduous** climb
   A easy
   B narrow
   C dangerous
   D strenuous

3. The **vivacious** singer
   A tired
   B well dressed
   C full of life
   D hopeless

4. A strange **malady**
   A illness
   B voice
   C humor
   D temper

5. To **transplant** the shrubbery
   A remove the roots
   B rake the leaves
   C take several cuttings
   D dig up and replant

6. An **exasperating** remark
   A soothing
   B annoying
   C courteous
   D foolish

7. To **wreak** vengeance
   A bring about
   B terminate
   C desire
   D fear

8. An **officious** person
   A courteous
   B stunning
   C meddlesome
   D very important

9. To **obliterate** the painting
   A continue
   B copy exactly
   C slightly change
   D wipe out

10. An **iniquitous** act
    A wicked
    B spontaneous
    C foolish
    D unnecessary

GO ON

11. **Cajoled** into a good mood
    A disgusted
    B changed
    C persuaded
    D forced

12. The **bumbling** old woman
    A dirty
    B awkward
    C loving
    D worried

13. To show **animosity**
    A curiosity
    B no interest
    C friendship
    D strong dislike

14. A few **superficial** wounds
    A profound
    B slight
    C deep
    D extensive

15. To **deliberate** for hours
    A discuss fully
    B extremely overjoyed
    C wait anxiously
    D argue unnecessarily

16. Several **mandatory** courses
    A semester
    B optional
    C required
    D elective

17. **Kindled** their interests
    A dampened
    B confused
    C distorted
    D aroused

18. The **dismal** weather forecast
    A dreary
    B sunny
    C bright
    D beautiful

19. His **condescending** tone
    A to uplift oneself
    B to be pleased
    C lowering oneself
    D to be undecided

20. The **ire** of the prisoners
    A delight
    B anger
    C sorrow
    D habits

STOP

WORDS AND THEIR MEANINGS

ACTIVITY: Choose the word that means the **same** as (or is the synonym for) the word in **bold** type. Fill in the circle next to the correct answer.

1. Some **stimulating** activities
   ① exciting
   ② forbidden
   ③ verbal
   ④ incomplete

2. An **odious** comment
   ① outrageous
   ② hateful
   ③ threatening
   ④ praiseworthy

3. Her **sober** remarks
   ① angry
   ② unnecessary
   ③ encouraging
   ④ serious

4. a **vicious** rumor
   ① malicious
   ② truthful
   ③ humorous
   ④ far-reaching

5. gave him a **cask** of wine
   ① bucket
   ② glass
   ③ barrel
   ④ liter

WORDS AND THEIR MEANINGS

ACTIVITY: Choose the word that means the **opposite** of (or is the antonym for) the word in **bold** type. Fill in the circle next to the correct answer.

6. the great **armada**
   ① one warship
   ② two tugboats
   ③ a fleet of ships
   ④ a group of sailboats

7. To **reimburse** your neighbor
   ① pay back
   ② lend to
   ③ say to
   ④ borrow from

8. **Relevant** information
   ① appropriate
   ② unrelated
   ③ correct
   ④ secret

9. To **prevaricate** is not honest.
   ① lie
   ② cheat
   ③ speak truthfully
   ④ fight

10. To **abstain** from drugs
    ① to do without
    ② overindulge
    ③ to refuse
    ④ to ignore

STOP

WORDS AND THEIR MEANINGS

ACTIVITY: Of the two words that **sound alike** (or are homonyms), circle the word that best completes the meaning in the sentence. If there are two blanks in a sentence, write the correct word in its corresponding blank.

1. I told my mother I really needed fifty _____ . **sense**   **cents**

2. We had to walk _____ the mud to the new house. **through**   **threw**

3. The prince is _____ to the English throne. **heir**   **air**

4. Our teacher found her new pen, _____ . **to**   **too**

5. Have you finished _____ math homework? **your**   **you're**

6. The opposite of wrong is _____ .
   I will _____ to you. **right**   **write**

7. The boys quickly ate _____ special pizzas. **four**   **for**

8. Katie is _____ the business envelopes. **sealing**   **ceiling**

9. _____ about time to begin your English research paper. **Its**   **It's**

10. Although Dr. Harrison has many _____ ,
    he always remains calm and full of _____ . **patience**   **patients**

11. The _____ stated their _____ or rules
    the first day of school. **principles**   **principals**

12. Will you choose Billy _____ Tommy for
    the captain? **ore**   **or**

13. If the sports event is next _____ , I will be
    too _____ to attend. **weak**   **week**

14. I have known _____ parents for at least
    seven years. **their**   **there**

15. If your _____ is over 135 pounds, you will
    have to _____ until tomorrow to wrestle. **wait**   **weight**

16. The bride and groom have decided that they
    want to marry at the _____ . We will have to
    _____ our plans and leave the courthouse
    to go to the church. **alter**   **altar**

STOP

ORIGIN OF WORDS

ACTIVITY: Read the meaning given for each word. Decide which present-day word comes from the original word. Circle the letter of the correct word.

1. Which word may have come from the Latin word **carricare,** meaning "an extra charge"?

   A. surcease   B. surplus   C. surcharge   D. surpass

2. Which word probably came from the Greek word **graphein,** relating to "write, draw"?

   A. polyester   B. polygraph   C. polysyllabic   D. polygon

3. Which word may have come from the Latin word **petere,** meaning "to seek, strive"?

   A. compose   B. complex   C. compel   D. compete

4. Which word probably came from the Latin word **construere,** meaning "to interpret wrongly"?

   A. misdeed   B. misfit   C. misconstrue   D. miscalculate

5. Which word may have come from the Greek word **phobos,** meaning "fear"?

   A. hydrophobia   B. hydrant   C. hydroplane   D. hydroponics

6. Which of these words probably comes from the Middle English word **fitten,** meaning "a person who is badly adjusted"?

   A. fitful   B. misfortune   C. misprint   D. misfit

7. Which word may have come from the Latin word **aevum,** meaning "of or relating to prehistoric times"?

   A. primeval   B. primer   C. primordial   D. prime

8. Which of these words probably comes from the French word **veiller,** meaning "to watch"?

   A. surmount   B. surveillance   C. surveyor   D. survive

CHOOSING THE CORRECT WORD

ACTIVITY: Read the paragraphs. Decide which word from each list best completes the meaning in the corresponding blank. Circle the letter next to the correct answer.

KWANZAA

Kwanzaa (KWAH-nzah), a seven-day festival from December 26 through January 1, is ____(1)____ by African-Americans. Kwanzaa, which is based upon the traditional African festivals that celebrate the harvest of the first crop, means "the first" or "the first fruits of the harvest." Kwanzaa is actually a nonreligious/nonpolitical celebration. The focus of the celebration is on ____(2)____ of living rather than on heroic figures.

The festival was ____(3)____ in 1966 by Dr. Maulana Karenga, a Los Angeles-based Black Studies professor, to increase cultural awareness of the African heritage and encourage seven qualities such as unity, self-determination, and cooperation in the black community. The ____(4)____ includes exchanging gifts and eating an African-style meal known as karamu (kah-RAH-moo). Each day of Kwanzaa a candle should be lit beginning with the black candle which is placed in the center of the candle holder. Candles are then lit alternately from left to right. Three green candles should be placed on the left, and three red candles should be placed on the right. Each day a principle should be recited when the candle is lit.

1. A. observed
   B. inspected
   C. detected
   D. surveyed

2. A. controls
   B. standards
   C. principles
   D. awareness

3. A. opened
   B. discontinued
   C. folded
   D. originated

4. A. function
   B. observance
   C. notice
   D. practice

STOP

CHOOSING THE CORRECT WORD

ACTIVITY: Read the paragraphs. Decide which word from each answer list best completes the meaning of the corresponding sentence. Circle the letter next to each correct answer.

SWEDEN

Sweden forms the eastern part of the Scandinavian peninsula. From the icy wastes of the Arctic, the country stretches south toward Denmark. There are mountains along the border with Norway, _____(1)_____ to lowlands along the coast. The long Baltic coastline is broken into many islands. In the center and the south of the country, there are a maze of lakes that were _____(2)_____ out of the landscape more than 10,000 years ago during the last Ice Age.

Sweden, one of the larger countries in Europe, is also one of the most sparsely populated. More than half the land is covered in forests of spruce and pine. These woodlands are home to wolves, bears, lynx, and red deer. They also provide timber for Sweden's highly profitable furniture and paper industries. The _____(3)_____ farmland in the south produces most of the country's food. Rich ore deposits in Lapland are another of the country's valuable resources. Rivers are _____(4)_____ to produce hydroelectric power for these and other industries. Sweden's wealth of natural resources has made it a _____(5)_____ country.

1. A forwarding
   B descending
   C driving
   D delaying

2. A gorged
   B granted
   C guarded
   D gouged

3. A fertile
   B barren
   C fruitless
   D frugal

4. A hinged
   B harnessed
   C hurried
   D helpless

5. A profound
   B populous
   C prosperous
   D unfortunate

STOP

WORDS AND THEIR MEANINGS

ACTIVITY: For each question, you are to decide which of the four answers is closest in meaning to the word in **bold type** above it. Circle the correct answer.

1. Our teacher read our class an **anonymous** poem.
   - A untitled
   - B mentioned
   - C unknown author
   - D not understood

2. Her **flippant** attitude annoyed my mother.
   - A cold and distant
   - B warm and friendly
   - C somewhat dignified
   - D disrespectful

3. Please **refrain** from talking in class.
   - A hold back
   - B begin now
   - C become tired
   - D become thirsty

4. The castle, built on top of the mountain, was **impregnable.**
   - A remote
   - B exposed
   - C invulnerable
   - D undefended

5. Our class was simply **stupefied** by the news.
   - A depressed
   - B astonished
   - C excited
   - D revived

6. Her **impulsive** nature gets her into trouble.
   - A carefully considered
   - B in hopes of a reward
   - C restrained
   - D spontaneous

7. Do you know what caused the **commotion?**
   - A an unexpected happening
   - B a very lengthy comedy
   - C noisy, disturbing activity
   - D a devastating fire

8. The teacher has been waiting for an **opportune** moment.
   - A unsuitable
   - B unfavorable
   - C appropriate
   - D inconvenient

9. She slowly **immersed** the old platter in the hot suds.
   - A submerged
   - B repaired
   - C decorated
   - D warmed

10. The governor made several **lucid** statements.
    - A complete
    - B confusing
    - C gloomy
    - D clear

STOP

CHAPTER THREE:

DEVELOPING SPELLING SKILLS

The purpose of this chapter is not to teach the process of spelling but rather to refine the student's ability to proof for misspelled words. Experience has shown that the spelling section of major achievement tests is geared toward the student choosing, from a series of words, the one word that is correctly spelled or, conversely, incorrectly spelled.

The exercises in this chapter have been carefully chosen to take the student step-by-step through the process of learning to proof for spelling errors with speed and accuracy. Please note that the worksheets in the final part of this chapter are based on formats the student will be exposed to on various standardized achievement tests. Feel free to use some or all of the formats as your situation requires.

ACTIVITY: Read the words in each exercise and look for a spelling mistake. In the answer rows, fill in the circle by the word with a mistake. If you do not find a mistake, mark your answer **No Mistakes**.

1. ○ a. chair
   ○ b. table
   ○ c. sofa
   ○ d. furnitere
   ○ e. No Mistakes

2. ○ a. fether
   ○ b. fur
   ○ c. father
   ○ d. far
   ○ e. No Mistakes

3. ○ a. division
   ○ b. multiplication
   ○ c. subtraction
   ○ d. adition
   ○ e. No Mistakes

4. ○ a. school
   ○ b. library
   ○ c. musseum
   ○ d. gymnasium
   ○ e. No Mistakes

STOP

FINDING THE MISSPELLED WORD

ACTIVITY: Many of the questions in this exercise contain spelling mistakes. Some do not have any mistakes at all. In the answer rows, fill in the circle next to the word that contains a mistake. If you do not find a mistake, mark your answer **No Mistakes.**

A. ① drawing
    ② outline
    ③ sketch
    ④ freight
    ⑤ No Mistakes

B. ① general
    ② lieutenant
    ③ capatan
    ④ sergeant
    ⑤ No Mistakes

C. ① sheet
    ② bedspread
    ③ matterial
    ④ mattress
    ⑤ No Mistakes

D. ① generus
    ② genuine
    ③ greedy
    ④ gracious
    ⑤ No Mistakes

E. ① television
    ② intertainment
    ③ amusement
    ④ recreation
    ⑤ No Mistakes

F. ① preacher
    ② devotion
    ③ religion
    ④ belief
    ⑤ No Mistakes

G. ① veterinarian
    ② bricklayer
    ③ criminial
    ④ accountant
    ⑤ No Mistakes

H. ① grammar
    ② history
    ③ mathmatics
    ④ science
    ⑤ No Mistakes

I. ① tournement
    ② league
    ③ colleague
    ④ associate
    ⑤ No Mistakes

J. ① stomach
    ② brain
    ③ showlder
    ④ ankle
    ⑤ No Mistakes

K. ① interfere
    ② hazardus
    ③ embarrass
    ④ specialize
    ⑤ No Mistakes

L. ① auxiliary
    ② recycled
    ③ deliberateion
    ④ fascinating
    ⑤ No Mistakes

GO ON

M.
① mischievious
② persuaded
③ scenic
④ arrangement
⑤ No Mistakes

S.
① unanimeous
② dictionary
③ provision
④ illustrated
⑤ No Mistakes

N.
① conscience
② nauseous
③ illustrated
④ millimeter
⑤ No Mistakes

T.
① archeology
② chauffeur
③ noticable
④ ignorance
⑤ No Mistakes

O.
① turquoise
② compelled
③ reciept
④ boulevard
⑤ No Mistakes

U.
① jugement
② fortunate
③ allowance
④ proposition
⑤ No Mistakes

P.
① occassionally
② donation
③ symbolic
④ conjunction
⑤ No Mistakes

V.
① emperor
② significant
③ evaporate
④ maturity
⑤ No Mistakes

Q.
① persuade
② oppertunity.
③ sympathy
④ biography
⑤ No Mistakes

W.
① rhinnocoeros
② weight
③ meanwhile
④ registered
⑤ No Mistakes

R.
① executive
② stationery
③ manuever
④ sabotage
⑤ No Mistakes

X.
① cereal
② dynamic
③ disregeard
④ rhythm
⑤ No Mistakes

STOP

FINDING THE MISSPELLED WORD

ACTIVITY: Look at each group of words and find the misspelled word. Fill in the circle that has the same letter as the misspelled word. Then, write the word correctly on the line.

1. a. climite   c. weather   ⓐ ⓑ ⓒ ⓓ _____
   b. season   d. misplaced

2. a. steamship c. submarine   ⓐ ⓑ ⓒ ⓓ _____
   b. chocolate d. yaht

3. a. riddle   c. question   ⓐ ⓑ ⓒ ⓓ _____
   b. wisdom   d. puzzel

4. a. alike   c. instrument ⓐ ⓑ ⓒ ⓓ _____
   b. familar   d. similar

5. a. book   c. magasine   ⓐ ⓑ ⓒ ⓓ _____
   b. report   d. newspaper

6. a. counterfeit c. leisure   ⓐ ⓑ ⓒ ⓓ _____
   b. beseiged   d. audience

7. a. evaporate c. absurd   ⓐ ⓑ ⓒ ⓓ _____
   b. silouette d. eclipse

8. a. banquet   c. quotation   ⓐ ⓑ ⓒ ⓓ _____
   b. mayonnaise d. distinquish

9. a. windsheild c. intestinal ⓐ ⓑ ⓒ ⓓ _____
   b. caravan   d. wrench

10. a. pavement c. disobedeint ⓐ ⓑ ⓒ ⓓ _____
    b. deceit   d. success

11. a. distres   c. impatient   ⓐ ⓑ ⓒ ⓓ _____
    b. sculpture d. lifeguard

12. a. influence c. banquet   ⓐ ⓑ ⓒ ⓓ _____
    b. circumstance d. deffective

13. a. obblige   c. dismissed   ⓐ ⓑ ⓒ ⓓ _____
    b. continent d. cubic

STOP

FINDING THE CORRECTLY SPELLED WORD

ACTIVITY: Fill in the bubble for the word that is spelled correctly and best completes the sentence.

1. The policemen have _____ evidence.
   - ○ A sufficient
   - ○ B suficient
   - ○ C sufficeint
   - ○ D suficiant

2. The landlord received a _____ for this month's rent.
   - ○ A remitance
   - ○ B remitence
   - ○ C remmittance
   - ○ D remittance

3. Please read directions when you try this new _____ .
   - ○ A solushun
   - ○ B solution
   - ○ C sollution
   - ○ D solucion

4. Robert admitted he had an unusual _____ dream.
   - ○ A recuring
   - ○ B reccuring
   - ○ C recurring
   - ○ D reccurring

5. Roxanne receives a _____ for every sale she makes.
   - ○ A commission
   - ○ B comission
   - ○ C commnision
   - ○ D comishion

6. JoAnne will probably be promoted to a _____ position.
   - ○ A manegerial
   - ○ B managariel
   - ○ C manegariel
   - ○ D managerial

7. Sandra's _____ in ecological issues led to her promotion.
   - ○ A envolviment
   - ○ B involvement
   - ○ C involvment
   - ○ D envolvement

8. Christine has been _____ at tennis.
   - ○ A proficient
   - ○ B profficeint
   - ○ C proficeint
   - ○ D profficant

9. My cousin is a _____ in the army.
   - ○ A leiutenant
   - ○ B lietenuant
   - ○ C lieutenant
   - ○ D lieutenent

10. The secretary _____ all of his phone calls.
    - ○ A inturcepted
    - ○ B intercepted
    - ○ C entercepted
    - ○ D enterrcepted

GO ON

11. The car is _____ to cause some trouble.
    - ○ A beggining
    - ○ B beginning
    - ○ C begining
    - ○ D biginning

12. The woman's _____ was greatly appreciated.
    - ○ A generousity
    - ○ B generrosity
    - ○ C generocity
    - ○ D generosity

13. Our city has three _____ under construction.
    - ○ A skyscrapers
    - ○ B skysrapars
    - ○ C skyscrapirs
    - ○ D skiscrappers

14. Can you _____ these two products at the same time?
    - ○ A mannufacture
    - ○ B manefacture
    - ○ C manufacture
    - ○ D manufakture

15. We cannot _____ John for the position.
    - ○ A reccommend
    - ○ B recomend
    - ○ C reccomend
    - ○ D recommend

16. Mrs. Cook took her dog to _____ school.
    - ○ A obedience
    - ○ B obeadience
    - ○ C obeadance
    - ○ D obediance

17. The teacher said that we could start our _____ .
    - ○ A expearment
    - ○ B experiment
    - ○ C experimant
    - ○ D experiement

18. I have earned enough _____ flyer miles.
    - ○ A freequent
    - ○ B freguent
    - ○ C frequent
    - ○ D ferquent

19. The Statue of Liberty is _____ of freedom.
    - ○ A cimbolic
    - ○ B cymbolic
    - ○ C symbolic
    - ○ D simbolic

20. My mother told me not to _____ with Tommy.
    - ○ A asociate
    - ○ B assocate
    - ○ C asocciate
    - ○ D associate

21. Mr. Drake is _____ for his traveling expenses.
    - ○ A reimbursed
    - ○ B reimberced
    - ○ C reimbersed
    - ○ D reimburced

22. Would you _____ the last two questions on this test?
    - ○ A elliminate
    - ○ B eliminat
    - ○ C eliminate
    - ○ D elimminate

STOP

FINDING THE MISSPELLED WORD

ACTIVITY: Read the following phrases. Three of the underlined words are spelled correctly. Find the phrase containing an underlined word that is **not** spelled correctly, and fill in the bubble next to that phrase.

1.
- ○ A wonderful <u>compliment</u>
- ○ B quiet <u>neighborhood</u>
- ○ C <u>expennsive</u> taste
- ○ D a quick <u>glance</u>

2.
- ○ A <u>bunches</u> of bananas
- ○ B ordered <u>yesterday</u>
- ○ C filled with <u>intrique</u>
- ○ D the other <u>culprit</u>

3.
- ○ A sense of <u>equality</u>
- ○ B a <u>unanimeous</u> decision
- ○ C <u>gullible</u> personality
- ○ D <u>acknowledge</u> my call

4.
- ○ A <u>charitible</u> event
- ○ B <u>humiliating</u> remark
- ○ C out of <u>necessity</u>
- ○ D <u>ineffective</u> on the job

5.
- ○ A lacks <u>patience</u>
- ○ B roll of <u>thundur</u>
- ○ C <u>arrogant</u> attitude
- ○ D <u>solemn</u> service

6.
- ○ A <u>geography</u> lesson
- ○ B my chosen <u>profession</u>
- ○ C <u>classification</u> of books
- ○ D <u>conventtional</u> wedding

7.
- ○ A western <u>hemisphere</u>
- ○ B <u>dreneched</u> in chocolate
- ○ C <u>economy</u> class ticket
- ○ D reached a <u>decision</u>

8.
- ○ A <u>anxiety</u> attack
- ○ B a clever <u>commedian</u>
- ○ C my road <u>atlas</u>
- ○ D physical <u>attraction</u>

9.
- ○ A <u>cunning</u> as a fox
- ○ B his loyal <u>teammates</u>
- ○ C cannot be <u>surpased</u>
- ○ D <u>confidential</u> information

10.
- ○ A <u>philosiphy</u> of life
- ○ B <u>exasperated</u> body builder
- ○ C <u>sentimental</u> values
- ○ D <u>antiseptic</u> mouthwash

STOP

CHAPTER FOUR:

ENHANCING READING COMPREHENSION

Learning to understand (or comprehend) what you read is one of the most important skills you will ever acquire. One certain way to enhance your reading comprehension is to create an image or picture in your mind as you read. In this chapter, several activities are presented that will improve your reading comprehension.

ACTIVITY: Read the following poem, "Silence," by Jeremy Hinds, and answer the questions that follow.

SILENCE

Jeremy Hinds

No sun rose to waken the world
   but a gust of the wind's breath
   rises rustling, the leafless trees moan and sway.
Grey sky hangs silent o'er the earth
   like mountains above a northland town   5
   with lodgings shut tight to stay the ice.
It looks with omnipotence upon the powerless land.
Waves are tossed, thrown, hurled upon the coasts,
   then breaking upon the solid stone one million years in the making.
Fold your sails; skeleton masts rise and fall,   10
   riding out His fury, praying for redemption,
   but in the end, all returns to silence.
Like a weak voice raised to tempt the truth
   crushed hard upon the stone of unquestionability.
Like a leash on the neck of a tundra wolf,   15
   broken are the threads of meaningless lives
   to fall away to the wastes.
Looking into the mirror, they see the vast, immeasurable desert,
   being but grains of sand, falling back.
In the end, silence prevails, as the world whimpers,   20
   and there's no bang left to be heard.

1. In line 11, the word **His** probably refers to what or whom, since it is capitalized?

     ○ A Sun   ○ B God   ○ C Waves   ○ D Earth

2. Read the last two lines. The expression "there's no bang left to be heard" may be an allusion to what theory that explains the creation of the world?

     ○ A Cosmic Dust Theory   ○ C Big Bang Theory
     ○ B Creation   ○ D Spontaneous Theory

3. Lines 4-6 contain a simile. To what is the sky compared?

     ○ A mountains   ○ B town   ○ C lodgings   ○ D ice

STOP

ACTIVITY: Read the following information by Heather Benson on rain forests, and then answer the questions on the next page.

Destruction of the Rain Forest

When thinking on the world's environmental problems, one's attention must be drawn to the destruction of the rain forest. The rain forest has been cut from around six million square miles to about three million square miles. Rain forests began to form about 140 million years ago, and it has taken man only a short time to destroy them. The destruction of the rain forests causes the loss of valuable plants and animal species, and this loss is directly related to man's needs and desires.

The destruction of the rain forests is mainly due to the human need for space and materials that are only found in this diverse **biome.** The destruction affects the world in environmental terms as well as economic terms. The rain forests provide timber, vanilla, cocoa, coffee and avocado. Also many fruits such as papaya, mango and bananas are native to these areas. Most areas are being cleared for cattle, farming and logging which are all human needs. In the case of rain forests, human needs seem to exceed environmental needs and so the destruction continues.

Rain forests provide living space to over fifty percent of the world's species of plants and animals. Rain forest destruction causes the loss of whole communities of species. Many communities have been destroyed before they can even be studied and observed scientifically. Any amount of disturbance can greatly alter the development of the species that inhabit the rain forest and the destruction has led to their extinction. In about 30 years, if the current rate continues, the tropical rain forests will disappear or be damaged to the point of no repair. This means that along with the loss of the rain forests there will also be the loss of millions of plants and animals.

The variety of plants and animals that can be found in the rain forest is unbelievable and so is their damaged status. One twenty-five acre plot of rain forest in Malaysia contains 750 species of trees while the entire tree population of the United States and Canada is only 700 species. One example of the effects on animal life is the Spix's macaw. This is a parrot native to northeast Brazil. These birds can cost $18,000 each because of their rare status. Thirty Spix's macaws are owned privately, but because of the rain forest destruction and the eradication of nesting sites, there is only one left in the wild. The sad part is that the one left in the wild has been unseen for several years.

Every person on the planet will be affected by rain forest destruction. If this process is not altered, the planet and the people will begin to feel the destruction of this important biome very soon.

GO ON ➤

QUESTIONS ON *"DESTRUCTION OF THE RAIN FORESTS"*

1. What percent of the world's species of plants and animals live in the rain forests?

   ○ A under 50%   ○ B 75%   ○ C 50%   ○ D over 50%

2. If rain forests continue to disappear at the rate at which they are in 1996, in about what year will rain forests have disappeared or will be damaged to the point of no repair?

   ○ A 2325   ○ B 2026   ○ C 2095   ○ D 2126

3. According to this article, what are some foods found in rain forests?

   ○ A cocoa, tea, coffee

   ○ B papaya, mango, orange

   ○ C bananas, avocado, vanilla

   ○ D avocado, coffee, apple

4. The Spix's macaw is a parrot native to Brazil, but because of rain forest destruction, there are only how many left in the wild?

   ○ A 1   ○ B 30   ○ C 18,000   ○ D 700

5. There are about how many different species of trees found in the United States?

   ○ A 700   ○ B 750   ○ C Not Given   ○ D 1450

6. Look at the word **biome** in the second paragraph. The word, as it is used, probably means which one of the following?

   ○ A microcosm   ○ C environment (land, climate, etc.)

   ○ B house and shelter   ○ D study of plants and animals

7. Because of their rare status, Spix's macaws are valued at $_____ each.

   ○ A $18,000   ○ B $1,800   ○ C $800   ○ D $80

STOP

ACTIVITY: Read the following story by Summer Bagwell, and then answer the questions that follow.

The Birthday

The rain was falling as Andie ran through her front door. She tossed her school books on the living room couch as the door slammed behind her. The rain and gloom outside matched her mood. Today was Andie's thirteenth birthday and no one had even remembered. Her family, friends, and classmates had not even mentioned the fact that this was her big day, the day she finally became a teenager.

"Well, if they can't remember something like my birthday, how can they be my real friends?" she said to herself. "Even my parents forgot about me."

She saw a note on the kitchen table that was scribbled rather hastily in her mother's handwriting. "Hey sweetheart," she read aloud, "we've gone to town for the afternoon. Do your homework and be good and we will see you later tonight."

Andie sat down in her chair and began to feel extremely sorry for herself. "If no one wants to remember my birthday, then I will just celebrate it by myself," she thought.

She remembered where she put the copy of her favorite movie, and she started down the stairs to her bedroom. She opened the door and turned on the lights to a chorus of "Surprise!" She gasped as she saw a large group of her friends and family smiling at her.

"So they didn't forget, after all," she thought with satisfaction and a big smile. "I knew they wouldn't."

1. If **irony** is a word that means the opposite of what one might expect, what is ironic about Andie's long-anticipated thirteenth birthday?
   - ○ A the weather is gloomy
   - ○ B she is sad and the weather is gloomy
   - ○ C she is happy but the weather is gloomy
   - ○ D she is sad because she is sick

2. In the note left to Andie, her mother stated that the family had gone where?
   - ○ A to the neighbor's house
   - ○ B to the grocery store
   - ○ C to a movie
   - ○ D to town

3. Look at the expression "and began to feel extremely sorry for herself." What is another word for "to feel sorry for oneself"?
   - ○ A sympathy
   - ○ B empathy
   - ○ C self-pity
   - ○ D compassion

4. To celebrate her birthday, Andie was going to do what?
   - ○ A call a friend
   - ○ B watch a movie
   - ○ C watch television
   - ○ D cry in her bedroom

STOP

ACTIVITY: Read the following original work, "Journey into Madness," by Jeremy Hinds. Then answer the questions that follow on the next page.

Journey into Madness

We rode hard for eighteen days, seldom resting or stopping for meals. The sky was grey, hanging ominously like a dark shadow about our heads. Driving northward, the last three days of our journey lay beneath the looming towers of the Keldors, a range of such evil repute that few roamed into their shadows. The steeds were nervous, but pressed on loyally, bearing us nearer Burg Rangor, the dark citadel buried deep within the heart of the Keldors.

As the terrain worsened, we took the last day afoot, leading our horses along the stony trails deeper into the black mountains. About midday (at what time I could not tell, for the sun never showed its face), the sky further darkened and rain poured upon us, soaking our souls, it seemed, and our spirits were low. Still onward we pressed, struggling to bear in mind the ultimate goal.

The sky was a black sheet of glass, shattered by lightning and shaken by the low-rumbling thunder. One of our steeds, terrified by the storm, bolted off, fast disappearing into the darkness. In the darkness in the distance, some among us believed we heard the beast cry out eerily, a terrified scream from the abysmal black landscape surrounding us. Some time later we arrived at the evil gate of Burg Rangor, standing like a dark portal to an infernal plain.

My recollections of that evil place are faint, all senses having been warped by that otherworldly malignance. We descended a long case of stairs, winding deep into the earth. Our horses were tethered in the courtyard above. Our torches burned dim, and the smoke from the pitch was stifling. Our sole purpose in continuing was to rid the land of the darkness buried herein.

We reached the floor of that black cavern and swallowed hard against the nausea which ensued. The stone floor was strewn with bones, and the stench of carrion choked our lungs. Shapeless masses twisted and writhed on the outskirts of our vision. The remainder of this ill-fated excursion is mostly lost to me, my mind having cast the dark memories out in a struggle to maintain my sanity. My companions were broken, cut down by unearthly blades and claws and dragged into the shadows. I ran for my life, stumbling up the stairs, and finally reaching the courtyard only to find the mounts part-devoured by some demonic force. Nine entered Burg Rangor, and I alone escaped with my life.

Winged beast soared high overhead as I ran blind with terror. My body fatigued, I collapsed along the path, having my senses about me only enough to crawl beneath a large stone before consciousness escaped me entirely.

Now I sit in silence, walk alone, and wait helplessly, knowing this darkness will spread like a disease until all of the earth is consumed. I alone gazed upon the infernal creatures and survived, but I know my days are numbered on this doomed Earth.

—Found in the library of the Mage Feldoranon
From the Journal of Rantok the Mad

GO ON

QUESTIONS ON *"JOURNEY INTO MADNESS"*

1. In the first paragraph, what are the Keldors?
   - ○ A demons
   - ○ B shadows
   - ○ C mountains
   - ○ D family of brute rulers

2. In the expression "hanging ominously like a dark shadow above our heads," what are some context clues that help to define the word ***ominously?***
   - ○ A hanging down
   - ○ B grey
   - ○ C our heads
   - ○ D dark shadow

3. How many people are on this expedition, and how many escape?
   - ○ A 9–1
   - ○ B 9–0
   - ○ C 10–1
   - ○ D 10–0

4. What was the reason for this expedition?
   - ○ A to capture the Keldors
   - ○ B to rid the land of darkness
   - ○ C to find the valuable treasure
   - ○ D to kill the demons

5. In the third paragraph, what is another word for ***steed?***
   - ○ A men
   - ○ B horse
   - ○ C companions
   - ○ D balloons

6. Imagery is a technique in writing where the writer employs words to create a picture in the reader's mind that appeals to the senses. Which of the following expressions appeals to the sense of smell?
   - ○ A ". . . stone floor was strewn with bones, . . . "
   - ○ B "Shapeless masses twisted and writhed . . ."
   - ○ C ". . . stench of carrion choked our lungs."
   - ○ D ". . . torches burned dim, . . ."

STOP

ACTIVITY: The following essay by Cam Case shows that writing an essay is not a complicated task. Read the following work, and then answer the questions that follow on the next page. Fill in the circle next to the correct answer.

The Components of an Essay

The complexity of the English language does not appear readily to lend itself to easy communication. With the many forms of written communication used to express ideas, it is almost a mind boggling decision to decide how one should go about relating ideas to others. The choices range from poetry to short stories, from novels to essays. Using this method, one should follow a simple plan to make one's ideas more easily presentable and the train of thought more logical.

The first place to start is the length of the paper. Although there is really no limit to how many words an essay can be, it is wise to use a minimum of five paragraphs. Five paragraphs include the first, or introductory, paragraph and the last, or concluding, paragraph. The three paragraphs in the middle, referred to as the supporting paragraphs, are where the writer really goes into detail expressing what the paper is really about.

The first paragraph can be about three to five sentences, though there is no fixed number. The first sentence should introduce what the writer will be presenting. This will then be carried through the next few sentences leading up to the last. This last sentence, called the thesis statement, is the single most important sentence in the entire paper. The thesis statement gives the reader the topic to be expounded upon in the body as well as the idea around which the essay revolves.

The body of the essay is to be put into order from the least important point (first paragraph of the body) to the most important (last paragraph of the body). This is also to be the order in which the points appear in the thesis statement. The length of these paragraphs should be at least five sentences. The first sentence of each supporting paragraph is called the topic sentence because it is this sentence which signals to the reader what the whole paragraph is about. The topic sentence is the most important sentence in each supporting paragraph. Then, the concluding sentence of each paragraph in the body does two things: it must end the thought of the paragraph, and it must provide easy transition into the next paragraph. The transition allows the reader to move through the paper smoothly.

The final paragraph, known as the conclusion, begins with a re-worded version of the thesis statement. This restated thesis can be a little more simplified than the original. The next sentences should provide the transition from the restated thesis to the last sentence of the essay. This last sentence should really get some attention, leaving the reader with something to think about.

GO ON ➡

QUESTIONS ON *"THE COMPONENTS OF AN ESSAY"*

1. What is the single most important sentence in the whole paper?
   - ○ A topic sentence
   - ○ B thesis statement
   - ○ C restated thesis statement
   - ○ D first sentence

2. What is the writer trying to accomplish in the supporting paragraphs?
   - ○ A conclude what the thesis says
   - ○ B confuse the reader with facts
   - ○ C express with detail what the thesis says
   - ○ D present what others think

3. In which paragraph does one find the thesis statement?
   - ○ A first supporting paragraph
   - ○ B last supporting paragraph
   - ○ C first (introductory) paragraph
   - ○ D last (concluding) paragraph

4. In the last two paragraphs of Cam's paper, he uses the word *transition.* What does the word mean as he uses it?
   - ○ A to move smoothly from one place to another
   - ○ B to use rhythm
   - ○ C to use a needless shift
   - ○ D to use a sudden break

5. A well-written essay is one that clearly expresses the writer's viewpoint on a particular topic. To express one's topic concisely, structure and form are important. If you were planning to write an essay on "Peer Pressure," and you broke down your thesis statement into four points, how many supporting paragraphs would your essay contain if you used the structure detailed in this paper?
   - ○ A 3   ○ B 6   ○ C 4   ○ D 5

STOP

ACTIVITY: Read the following story by Bunja Rungruang, and then answer the questions that follow on the next page. Fill in the circle next to the correct answer.

A Mother's Day Card

A flattened and withering daffodil was dangling off the card I had made my Auntie Tate for Mother's Day. When I turned the corner near our house, I saw her sitting in her old rocker. I put the card back into my pocket before I got to the yard. When she saw me, she raised the cloth she was embroidering and waved it toward me.

"How was school?" Auntie Tate asked.

"All right," I said. "I like everything but the parents' reading classes. I never have anyone to read with."

"I don't want any child teaching me to read," she said. "The young should learn from the old, not the other way. Cutting cane was the only thing for a Haitian girl to do when I was your age."

Whenever she was sad, Auntie Tate would tell about the sugarcane fields, where she and my mother worked when they were children. They saw exhausted workers slice open their own flesh with big machetes. My grandfather died in these fields.

I was going to sneak the Mother's Day card under Auntie's pillow, but the way her face drooped into her palms made me want to give it to her right then. I dug into my pocket and handed her the card. She took it, forced the daffodil into place, and handed it back.

"Not this year," she said. "It's not mine. It's your mother's."

I knew my mother only from a picture. As a child, I had imagined my mother to be Erulie, the Haitian goddess of love, perfect in every way. However, I had lived with Auntie for all of nine years. She was my mother. I refused to stay with the lady in the picture. She left me once, and I will not allow her to do it again.

QUESTIONS ON *"A MOTHER'S DAY CARD"*

1. Where did Auntie Tate grow up?
   - ○ A United States
   - ○ B Mexico
   - ○ C Haiti
   - ○ D Nassau

2. How does Auntie Tate feel about education?
   - ○ A the old can learn from the young
   - ○ B the young can teach the old
   - ○ C the old and young can learn together
   - ○ D the young should learn from the old

3. What was inside the Mother's Day card?
   - ○ A a message of love
   - ○ B a daffodil
   - ○ C a message to her mother
   - ○ D a piece of cloth

4. How could the narrator tell when her Auntie Tate was sad?
   - ○ A Auntie Tate would look sad
   - ○ B Auntie Tate would talk about her father
   - ○ C Auntie Tate would talk about the sugarcane fields
   - ○ D Auntie Tate would not talk to anyone

5. Who was the narrator's mother?
   - ○ A Erulie
   - ○ B Auntie Tate
   - ○ C Erline
   - ○ D Not Given

STOP

ACTIVITY: Read the following original story by Zac Plumstead. Then answer the questions that follow on the next page. Fill in the circle next to the correct answer.

Evan's Song

"Bang!" shouted Evan, with his hand fixed into the shape of a pistol pointed at his head. "I'm about to end it all!" he said, while sitting on his bedroom floor. With tears rolling down his cheeks, Evan plugged his guitar into his amplifier and let loose a series of nasty blues licks.

Evan's music was his way of releasing his emotions. At school Evan was a so-called "weirdo" and the butt of many jokes. His music let him release all of the anger he had bottled up inside. His music was his medicine.

"Tomorrow," said Evan, "tomorrow, I'll show 'em." Tomorrow the school would be having its annual "Senior Show," and Evan had a surprise for his fellow classmates.

Evan arrived at school early the next morning so that he could set up his guitar and amplifier in the school's gymnasium for his performance later that morning. Word of his scheduled performance quickly spread throughout the school. Everyone found the whole thing very amusing. "What's that idiot going to do? Is he going to play us a song on his guitar?" someone said laughing.

The announcement was made for everyone to report to the gym for the show. Evan sat alone in the corner of the gym awaiting his performance. His was to be the last performance of the show, so Evan decided to play a song he had written entitled "Swan Song." Evan wrote this song to release his haunting thoughts of suicide.

Finally, his time came. Without saying a word, Evan walked to his guitar and plugged it into his amplifier. An eerie silence fell over the entire crowd as Evan stood motionless holding his guitar. He closed his eyes and began to play his heart out. The crowd stared in awe as Evan unleashed the song's solo. Evan, playing with his eyes closed, brought the song to a close. The students who had once made fun of him were now on their feet cheering. After the cheering stopped, Evan slowly walked to a nearby microphone and with a smile said, "You're welcome!"

GO ON

QUESTIONS ON *"EVAN'S SONG"*

1. How does Evan release his frustrations?
   - ○ A drinking
   - ○ B suicide
   - ○ C fighting
   - ○ D music

2. "Evan was a so-called weirdo and the butt of many jokes." What is the author trying to portray?
   - ○ A Evan dressed rather funny
   - ○ B being different is not good
   - ○ C examples of peer pressure
   - ○ D everyone who plays a guitar is weird

3. Evan wrote "Swan Song" for what reason?
   - ○ A to show that he could play the guitar
   - ○ B to rid himself of thoughts of suicide
   - ○ C to play for the student body
   - ○ D to carry out his plan of suicide

4. At the end of the story, Evan "with a smile said, 'You're welcome!'" What does the author of the story actually mean with "You're welcome"?
   - ○ A Reader will determine what Evan means.
   - ○ B Evan is being sarcastic with his newfound popularity.
   - ○ C This is Evan's last comment before his suicide.
   - ○ D Evan is sincere to his "new" friends.

STOP

CHAPTER FIVE:

EXPLORING LANGUAGE MECHANICS

It is important to learn how to communicate in written language. Through proper mechanical usage, we can better understand and relate to each other. When we study and understand any language, expression in written form becomes easier. Therefore, we must learn and understand any language in its written form if we are to live and work together successfully.

The purpose of this chapter is to develop and improve mechanical skills. The exercises have been chosen with emphasis on punctuation and capitalization. Working through these exercises, you can improve your achievement scores as well as have a sense of pride and confidence in your ability to use language.

PUNCTUATION

ACTIVITY: Read the following sentences. Fill in the circle by the mark of punctuation that best completes the sentence. If no marks are needed, fill in the circle by the word **None.**

1. Amaia are you going to Spain this summer?

    ○ ,   ○ :   ○ ;   ○ None

2. The following students may go to the library to check out a book Jan, Jorge, Adam, and Melanie.

    ○ ;   ○ :   ○ .   ○ None

3. Mr. Williams said, "Tonight's performance will begin at 8:00.

    ○ .   ○ :   ○ "   ○ None

4. Help I don't understand how to do this history homework.

    ○ ,   ○ .   ○ !   ○ None

5. Last summer my family and I went on vacation to Orlando Florida.

    ○ ,   ○ :   ○ ;   ○ None

STOP

PUNCTUATION AND CAPITALIZATION

ACTIVITY: Read the following sentences. Circle the letter next to the sentence that is written correctly.

1. A The traffic on highway 67 is heavy at times.
   B Students at the Middle School were invited.
   C You can buy fresh bread daily at The Market, a southern regional restaurant.
   D The bismarck, a very famous battleship, went down in 1941.

2. A My family is moving to the west in the Summer.
   B Yesterday, our class studied an article in time magazine.
   C "Everyone bring your coats," said the coach, "And be on time."
   D World War II was fought in Europe.

3. A Furthermore, coach Wisener said she was proud of us.
   B I knew that tony needed the job, so I asked.
   C What are you planning to do for New Years Eve?
   D We stayed at the Wayside Inn in Concord.

4. A On our visit to new Hampshire, Dad fainted.
   B Our Mexican-american friends have gone home.
   C The challenger accident upset many Americans.
   D The train ran arail near the county line.

5. A By the way she's finished with the book.
   B If I can't, I can't.
   C Before Thomas arrived at miles Grocery, the rain had begun.
   D Aunt Cleo will you please read this poem slowly.

6. A Mohammed is returning with his dad to cairo.
   B Pam's favorite kind of food is Italian.
   C Lets go to the game and cheer for our team.
   D I'm going to the Gym to workout for the third time this week.

7. A Is anyone interested.
   B The best time to visit is during the Rainy Season.
   C Gail has moved with her parents to Phoenix, Arizona.
   D If hed study harder, his grades would improve.

8. A He said to go north one mile and turn left.
   B Jason shouted, "it's your turn to wash the car."
   C "Don't get me wrong, said the principal, "Because I make mistakes too."
   D She's practicing to participate in the Summer olympics.

9. A Jo yelled "Ouch."
   B Doesnt that count also?
   C Yes, I'm going with her.
   D "No,' said the man.

STOP

PUNCTUATION AND CAPITALIZATION

ACTIVITY: Read the following sentences. Circle the letter next to the sentence that is written correctly.

1. A No he hasn't been here.
   B Jamie bought a car, a sofa, and a chair.
   C They did'nt know the answer.
   D Johannes asked, "what is the capital of Utah?"

2. A Lee said that "we should go to the circus."
   B Were going to the library after lunch.
   C It is satisfactory with me.
   D Mrs. Baron the assistant, works very hard.

3. A I looked there for the ring, did you find it?
   B "Has anyone found it?" asked Bob.
   C "No, said Tera.
   D I found three marbles a ring, and a glove.

4. A Mr. Hinds the school janitor; swept the halls.
   B Looking for the books; Matthew found his coat.
   C well be home around 7:00.
   D Devin asked, "What is the name of the tiger?"

5. A my uncle Bob owns several goats.
   B Our trip to malaysia was most exciting.
   C Do you own a boat.
   D Aunt Agnes is coming to our house for lunch.

6. A Our tour of the nasa facility was the most exciting part of the trip.
   B Sara and I enjoyed our trip to the Grand Canyon.
   C Next monday night we are going skiing.
   D The french fries at my Aunt's house are good.

7. A My favorite planet to study is saturn.
   B Will you be home next Saturday night.
   C Rafael, who is from Brazil, is in my class.
   D In Brazil, Rafael can swim in january.

8. A Did you see all the Rocks that Zac has in his collection?
   B Brax said, "that he had seen the collection."
   C The Teacher was invited to read the acceptance speech.
   D He'll present the award again this year.

9. A Have you ever traveled interstate highway #1?
   B Dad's birthday is on valentine's day.
   C Grandmother Livingston lives at 86 Oak Street.
   D Michul's polish friend Arek was at the Welcome party.

STOP

PUNCTUATION AND CAPITALIZATION

ACTIVITY: Read the following sentences carefully and circle the letter next to the line that is **incorrect.** If there are no mistakes, circle the letter by **No Mistakes.**

1. A   My favorite time of the
   B   year is Fall when all the
   C   leaves turn vibrant colors.
   D   No Mistakes

2. A   A very beautiful National Park
   B   in Asheville, North Carolina,
   C   is Pisgah National Park.
   D   No Mistakes

3. A   One day I would like to visit
   B   South Dakota, where
   C   my friend Peggy lives.
   D   No Mistakes

4. A   The magazine that Heronda
   B   enjoys reading in her spare
   C   time is called ebony.
   D   No Mistakes

5. A   As we hiked along the rough
   B   mountain trail, Uncle Bud yelled,
   C   "this brings back good memories."
   D   No Mistakes

6. A   Michael, who lives down the
   B   street, has an Aunt leslie who
   C   has been to China three times.
   D   No Mistakes

7. A   John and his sister joanne are
   B   planning to take swimming
   C   lessons during the summer.
   D   No Mistakes

8. A   In our class today we learned
   B   that venus is a very hot planet
   C   and is close to Earth.
   D   No Mistakes

9. A   When we stopped and asked
   B   the policeman for directions, he
   C   said to go south one mile.
   D   No Mistakes

10. A   "Don't forget to put your
    B   name on your paper," the teacher
    C   said, "and take your time.
    D   No Mistakes

STOP

PUNCTUATION AND CAPITALIZATION

ACTIVITY: Read the following letter and identify the mistakes by circling the letter of the line on which the mistake occurs.

---

1. A   510 Green Street
   - B   Yankton, SD, 57078

   - C   January 8, 1996
   - D   No Mistakes

2. A   The Book Factory
   - B   555 Fifth Avenue
   - C   New York, NY 10022

   - D   Dear Manager;

3. A   I have enjoyed reading ***I Know Why the Caged Bird Sings,***
   - B   by Maya Angelou and I am now preparing to do some research on
   - C   Ms. Angelou, her book, and her poetry.
   - D   No Mistakes

4. A   My seventh grade class has read and discussed her book.
   - B   I really liked it, and I want to know more about her life and works.
   - C   Do you have any research material I can purchase.
   - D   No Mistakes

5. A   Thank you very much for your help.

   - B   Sincerely yours.

   - C   Peggy Green

   - D   No Mistakes

STOP

PUNCTUATION AND CAPITALIZATION

ACTIVITY: Read the following passages, paying close attention to the underlined segments on the numbered lines. From the lists that follow, choose the answer that correctly completes the sentences and circle the letter beside it.

       Desmond and his friends sometimes go over to Guntersville

1.   <u>lake? They</u> enjoy swimming and relaxing there when they

2.   are not in school. <u>However if</u> they go to the lake to swim,

3.   <u>Desmonds mother</u> says they must all swim together. If they go

4.   to the lake to <u>relax they</u> usually take drinks and sandwiches

    and books to read.

1. A lake. They
   B Lake, They
   C Lake. They
   D No Mistakes

2. A However: if
   B However, if
   C however, if
   D No Mistakes

3. A Desmond's mother
   B Desmond's Mother
   C Desmonds, mother
   D No Mistakes

4. A relax, They
   B relax; they
   C relax, they
   D No Mistakes

STOP

PUNCTUATION AND CAPITALIZATION

ACTIVITY: Read the underlined segment of each of the following sentences, and then circle the answer that correctly completes the sentence.

1. Her grandfather said, "Did you think to feed the <u>dog.</u>

   A dog?   B dog"?   C dog?"   D No Mistakes

2. "<u>Dont</u> they have the combination to your locker?" Amanda's father said.

   A Don't   B "Don't   C "Dont,   D No Mistakes

3. "Take your coat and gloves," said Maria's <u>grandmother, and</u> don't forget to button your coat."

   A grandmother, "and   B grandmother and   C grandmother and"
   D No Mistakes

ACTIVITY: Read the following passages, paying close attention to the underlined segments on the numbered lines. From the lists that follow, choose the answer that correctly completes the sentences.

   Zac and Eleanor really enjoyed their visit to Greece last

4. <u>spring. However,</u> it was sad that their friends from school could

5. not go. In <u>Athens the capital</u> they saw the Parthenon and the

6. Acropolis, some of the oldest sites in Greece. <u>Eleanors excitement</u> to be at the Acropolis was so overwhelming that she used three rolls of

7. film while she was there. On the way back to the <u>hotel, however Zac</u> dropped his camera and lost his strap, but luckily the camera did not break.

   4. A Spring. However   6. A Eleanor's Excitement
       B spring, however   B Eleanor's excitement
       C spring: However,   C Eleanors, excitement
       D No Mistakes   D No Mistakes

   5. A Athens, the Capital,   7. A hotel, however,
       B athens: the capital   B Hotel, however,
       C Athens, the capital,   C hotel; however,
       D No Mistakes   D No Mistakes

STOP

CHAPTER SIX:

IMPROVING LANGUAGE USAGE

We learn how to communicate better with one another by exploring and improving our language skills. We also learn to appreciate and understand people better through the proper usage and expression of words.

The purpose of this chapter is to help you learn to express your ideas correctly and more effectively. The exercises have been carefully selected with emphasis on language usage and expression. Diligently working through these sample exercises will improve your language achievement scores and help you considerably in your self-expression.

RECOGNIZING STANDARD ENGLISH

ACTIVITY: In the following sentences, fill in the bubble of the letter of the word that correctly completes each sentence.

1. Jim _____ have all of his math homework completed yet.

    ○ A don't   ○ B will   ○ C doesn't   ○ D has

2. One of the girls _____ in the competition for exactly three days.

    ○ A were   ○ B was   ○ C weren't   ○ D am

3. The young man prepared the delicious meal _____ .

    ○ A hisself   ○ B herself   ○ C themself   ○ D himself

4. Mohammed has _____ a good job in his English class this semester.

    ○ A done   ○ B did   ○ C doing   ○ D do

5. All the letters he has _____ have been returned this week.

    ○ A wrote   ○ B write   ○ C writing   ○ D written

6. I _____ my back swing for the match on Thursday.

    ○ A has been practicing   ○ C have been practicing
    ○ B ain't been practicing   ○ D have been practiced

STOP

RECOGNIZING STANDARD ENGLISH

ACTIVITY: Read the following sentences, and then fill in the circle of the sentence that is written correctly.

1. ○ A Me and Jason are going to the movie.
   ○ B It's wrote in French.
   ○ C Her car rides more smoother than mine.
   ○ D He is the tallest person in the class.

2. ○ A Jorge were in this country for one year.
   ○ B Miss Usher divided the books between Jeremy and me.
   ○ C What is the seventh grade girls doing tonight?
   ○ D I didn't never know her name.

3. ○ A Chip ran more quick than Len.
   ○ B Jonathan is the quicker boy in the group of 50.
   ○ C Michael, however, is quicker than Jason.
   ○ D Karisa is the most quickest of all girls.

4. ○ A Each of the girls was given an apple.
   ○ B All the boys is given an orange.
   ○ C The teacher was give a grapefruit.
   ○ D The principal he was given a tangerine.

5. ○ A The boy hisself ran all the errands.
   ○ B The principal encouraged the students to do the work theirselves.
   ○ C Everyone should do his or her own work.
   ○ D The people cheered himself for their hard work.

6. ○ A The water flowed rapid down the river.
   ○ B The water on that river is more swifter than on that one.
   ○ C Have you ever saw that newly released movie?
   ○ D The water flows more rapidly in some places on the Chattanooga River than it does on the Mississippi.

7. ○ A The play didn't last any longer than the movie.
   ○ B I am not no more tired today than I was yesterday.
   ○ C He is the boy, which moved here from Denver, Colorado.
   ○ D Alana she is the one whom is coming to speak to us.

8. ○ A Whom was the guest speaker for your class today?
   ○ B This is she speaking.
   ○ C Joseph is not never at home.
   ○ D Jake, who live on Pratt Lane, is a golden retriever.

STOP

CHOOSING A SUBJECT

ACTIVITY: Read the following sentences, and then fill in the circle of the answer that is the correct simple subject of the sentence.

1. There are twelve red apples on the kitchen countertop.
   ○ A There   ○ B twelve   ○ C apples   ○ D countertop

2. Although Alex isn't in the eighth grade, he can still participate in the game.
   ○ A Alex   ○ B eighth   ○ C grade   ○ D he

3. On Monday morning we are having a meeting in the new library.
   ○ A Monday   ○ B we   ○ C library   ○ D meeting

4. Sam, Nellie, and Major will be in town on Saturday morning.
   ○ A Sam, Nellie   ○ C Sam, Nellie, Major
   ○ B Nellie, Major   ○ D town

5. I would go to the football game Friday night if Heather would go.
   ○ A I   ○ B Heather   ○ C game   ○ D if

CHOOSING A VERB

ACTIVITY: Read the following sentences, and then fill in the circle of the answer that is the verb (predicate) of the sentence.

6. All of the seventh and eighth graders are going to the dance.
   ○ A are   ○ C all
   ○ B are going   ○ D are going to

7. On the birthday cake were planted thirteen red and white candles.
   ○ A planted   ○ B were   ○ C on   ○ D were planted

8. Summer and Celeste don't always miss the basketball game.
   ○ A don't miss   ○ C do miss
   ○ B don't always   ○ D miss

9. Tonight I am wearing a new blue suit and colorful tie.
   ○ A am wearing   ○ B am   ○ C wearing   ○ D Tonight

10. Will you read this book and discuss it with the class by next Tuesday?
    ○ A will read   ○ C will
    ○ B read, discuss   ○ D will read, discuss

STOP

RECOGNIZING STANDARD ENGLISH

ACTIVITY: After you have read the following sentences, fill in the circle of the letter next to the line that contains a mistake. If there is no mistake, fill in the circle that reads **No Mistakes.**

1. A ○ Josh meaned for the letter to be
   B ○ sent to his grandmother. She
       lives in Athens, Tennessee,
   C ○ not Athens, Georgia.
   D ○ No Mistakes

2. A ○ The eighth grade class is planning
   B ○ a field trip to the space museum.
   C ○ Let's us take cokes and chips.
   D ○ No Mistakes

3. A ○ The girls gathers every Saturday
   B ○ afternoon to play soccer. The
   C ○ boys gather to watch them.
   D ○ No Mistakes

4. A ○ Martin Luther King, Jr., was a
   B ○ great civil rights leader in the
   C ○ 1960s. Did you no that?
   D ○ No Mistakes

5. A ○ We read *Animal Farm*
   B ○ in the eighth grade. We
   C ○ learned that sheep are the most
       stupidest of the animals.
   D ○ No Mistakes

6. A ○ With a lot of counseling, the boy
   B ○ began to ask hisself many
   C ○ questions about what he had done.
   D ○ No Mistakes

7. A ○ Last summer my family and I
   B ○ went out West on a long vacation.
   C ○ It was then I realized that New
       Mexico is east of Arizona.
   D ○ No Mistakes

8. A ○ My grandmother is learning me
   B ○ to make biscuits from real flour,
   C ○ not from a mix. I enjoy cooking.
   D ○ No Mistakes

9. A ○ Amber is in my English class. She
   B ○ moved here three years ago, and
   C ○ she ain't been absent one day.
   D ○ No Mistakes

10. A ○ Grandpa said they were the best
    B ○ sugar cookies he had ever ate.
    C ○ Grandma knows how to cook.
    D ○ No Mistakes

11. A ○ Kevin's younger brother is smaller
    B ○ than Matthew's. Matthew's older
    C ○ sister is taller than Kevin.
    D ○ No Mistakes

12. A ○ You're going to see
    B ○ your brother graduate
    C ○ from college, aren't you?
    D ○ No Mistakes

13. A ○ Rebecca is always kind to her
    B ○ teachers, and she don't ever
    C ○ mistreat her friends and family.
    D ○ No Mistakes

14. A ○ Since Nathan has rode a horse
    B ○ all his life, he was chosen to be
    C ○ the leader on the summer trail
        ride.
    D ○ No Mistakes

STOP

EXPRESSING AN IDEA

ACTIVITY: In the following sentences, circle the letter of the sentence that **best expresses the idea.**

1. A   Dad's sister, who is younger than he, will be here to babysit us.
   B   Dad's sister, who is younger than he and knows how to babysit, will be here to babysit.
   C   Dad's younger sister will be here to babysit us.
   D   Younger than he and experienced in babysitting, Dad's sister will be here to babysit us.

2. A   Darwin prefers the plain ham sandwich without the added cheese, fresh tomato, leafy lettuce, and hot onions.
   B   A plain ham sandwich without the added cheese, fresh tomato, leafy lettuce, and hot onions is what Darwin prefers.
   C   Although Darwin likes ham sandwiches, he prefers the plain ham sandwich without the added cheese, fresh tomato, leafy lettuce, and hot onions.
   D   Darwin prefers a plain ham sandwich without cheese, tomato, lettuce, and onions.

3. A   Since I have been to them several times and I enjoyed myself every time I was there, I plan to conduct tours and take people around to all the historic sites.
   B   Since I have been to them several times and enjoyed myself, I plan to conduct tours to all the historic sites.
   C   Traveling to them several times and I enjoyed myself every time, I plan to conduct tours and take people around to all the historic sites.
   D   I plan to conduct tours and take people to all the historic sites because I have been to them several times and I enjoyed myself each time.

CHOOSING THE CORRECT WORD

ACTIVITY: Read the following sentences, and then circle the letter of the word or phrase that best completes each sentence.

4. Jan felt a little strange when he _____ in the classroom yesterday.
   A walk   B walked   C walking   D was walked

5. Alice Walker _____ the book *The Color Purple.*
   A has written   B written   C write   D has wrote

6. Although Scott is tall, he is not the _____ boy in the school.
   A most tallest   B more taller   C taller   D tallest

7. Mrs. Snow _____ to be here tomorrow at 9:00 A.M. to read the story.
   A is suppose   B is supposed   C will supposing   D had supposing

STOP

RECOGNIZING STANDARD ENGLISH

ACTIVITY: Read the following paragraph, and then answer the
questions that follow by circling the letter of the best answer.

(1) The weatherman had predicted that we might get a little snow,
even though we live in the South. (2) Then on Monday afternoon the
temperature dropped quickly and the snow began falling. (3) I talked
with my cousin on the phone Sunday night and <u>everyone</u> in Seattle
<u>was</u> doing great. (4) By midnight on Monday, we had iced roads with
seven inches of snow. (5) Because the roads were hazardous with icy
conditions, school was canceled Tuesday, Wednesday, and Thursday.
(6) On Friday <u>we was back</u> in school, and the storm had moved up the
east coast. (7) However, by Thursday afternoon, the <u>sun come</u> out and
began melting the ice and snow, even our fat, handsome snowman.

1. Which of the following sentences would be the best topic sentence for
   the paragraph?
   A It was a much needed vacation from school.
   B Everyone was happy to see so much snow.
   C It was a bad snowstorm for our area.
   D I had never seen so much ice in my life.

2. Which sentence should be omitted from this paragraph?

   A 1   B 5   C 2   D 3

3. Which sentence should be the closing sentence?

   A 6   B 5   C 4   D 7

4. In sentence 6, which is the correct way to write the underlined part?

   A I were back   C you was back
   B we were back   D No Change

5. In sentence 3, which is the correct way to write the underlined part?

   A everyone were   C everyone aren't
   B everyone am   D No Change

6. In sentence 7, which is the correct way to write the underlined part?

   A sun comes   C sun had come
   B sun came   D No Change

STOP

COMBINING SENTENCES

ACTIVITY: Read the following **bold sentences**, and then circle the letter of the sentence which is the best combination of the ideas presented.

1. **Everyone is going to see the play *A Raisin in the Sun*. *A Raisin in the Sun* has also been remade into a movie.**

   A   Everyone is going to see the play *A Raisin in the Sun*, which has also been made into a movie.

   B   Since everyone is going to see the play *A Raisin in the Sun*, it has also been remade into a movie.

   C   Everyone is going to see the play *A Raisin in the Sun*; therefore, it has also been remade into a movie.

   D   As everyone is going to see the play *A Raisin in the Sun*, it has also been remade into a movie.

2. **Josh was having some difficulty in his math class. Mrs. Haynes decided that he needed a tutor.**

   A   Josh was having some difficulty in his math class; nevertheless, Mrs. Haynes decided that he need a tutor.

   B   Until Josh was having some difficulty in his math class, Mrs. Haynes decided that he needed a tutor.

   C   Since Josh was having some difficulty in his math class, Mrs. Haynes decided that he needed a tutor.

   D   Before Josh was having some difficulty in his math class, Mrs. Haynes decided that he needed a tutor.

3. **Seth practiced water skiing everyday after school. Seth practiced water skiing on the lake near his house.**

   A   Because Seth practiced water skiing everyday after school, he practiced on the lake near his house.

   B   If Seth practiced water skiing everyday after school, he practiced water skiing on the lake near his house.

   C   Practicing water skiing everyday after school, Seth was on the lake near his house.

   D   Seth practiced water skiing everyday after school on the lake near his house.

STOP

DEVELOPING THE TOPIC SENTENCE

ACTIVITY: After reading the following topic sentences, choose the sentence that **best develops** each topic sentence.

1. Through her novel *To Kill a Mockingbird*, Harper Lee exposed racism and bigotry in the South in the United States.
   - ○ A Harper Lee was brought up in Alabama, but spent some time as an adult in New York.
   - ○ B The main characters in her novel are Scout, who is the narrator, and Jem, Scout's brother.
   - ○ C She exposed the bigotry and even the hatred of law-abiding and church-attending citizens.
   - ○ D Calpurnia was the housekeeper for Scout and Jem. She played a motherly role for them since their mother was dead.

2. The biggest island of Hawaii is rather unique with its many different types of terrain.
   - ○ A It is fun to visit the state because the temperature is always pleasant and there are so many things to see.
   - ○ B The terrain on the island can vary from desertlike to a small rain forest within a relatively short distance.
   - ○ C Most of the days are sunny and warm; however, it rains a lot at night.
   - ○ D On one of the islands, one can see tremendous amounts of mostly black lava of previous volcanic eruptions.

3. Maya Angelou, the African-American woman who read her poem at President Clinton's inauguration in 1992, has written poetry and novels which have contributed to the ever-expanding dimension of American literature.
   - ○ A Maya Angelou and President Clinton both come from the state of Arkansas.
   - ○ B In her novel *I Know Why The Caged Bird Sings*, Angelou gives an autobiographical account of her early life.
   - ○ C Students enjoy reading her poetry because she writes on a level which is easily understood.
   - ○ D Her writings reflect a need for all Americans to take a look within themselves and find a way for all of us to work and live together.

STOP

READING THE PARAGRAPH

ACTIVITY: Read the following paragraphs, and fill in the circle of the numbered sentence that does **not** belong.

1. 1. The crow is a very clever bird. 2. When the crow is trained, it makes an amusing pet; however, many states offer bounties for crows because they steal and do damage to crops. 3. It has been discovered through scientific research that while the spider's bite is poisonous, it is not apt to cause death. 4. Men have been hunting crows for years, but today there are more crows than ever before. 5. In the face of attack, the crow's survival is due to cooperation.

   A. Sentence 1   B. Sentence 2   C. Sentence 3   D. Sentence 5

2. 1. Pepper was among our earliest spices. 2. It has played both a political and social role as a spice. 3. A long time ago it was considered an appropriate gift for royalty to give and to receive. 4. Many times people used pepper to pay their taxes. 5. The tables and chairs were rearranged in the dining room. 6. Ransoms were once even paid in amounts of pepper.

   A. Sentence 1   B. Sentence 2   C. Sentence 4   D. Sentence 5

3. 1. The porcupine is one animal that fights back. 2. Prairie dogs, which are not actually dogs, make their homes underground in holes they dig. 3. The burrows are usually ten to fifteen feet long. 4. These animals create great colonies because they dig their holes closer together. 5. Rattlesnakes and owls occasionally use prairie dog holes for their homes. 6. Rattlesnakes, owls, and prairie dogs sometimes live together.

   A. Sentence 1   B. Sentence 3   C. Sentence 4   D. Sentence 6

4. 1. Hurricanes are huge circles of wind. 2. During battle, the enemy was often able to intercept radio messages. 3. They are formed around calm areas amid the trade winds in the Atlantic. 4. The trade winds force the hurricanes westward from the doldrums. 5. It is believed that hurricanes build up more power than any other force in nature. 6. As much as one trillion pounds of pressure can be built up by a tropical hurricane.

   A. Sentence 1   B. Sentence 2   C. Sentence 3   D. Sentence 6

STOP

CHAPTER SEVEN:

UTILIZING MATHEMATICAL CONCEPTS AND ESTIMATION

Achievement tests always place special emphasis on how well students understand the number system and the terms and operations used in math. In recognition of this fact, Chapter 7 introduces the student to these skills in a typical test-taking situation.

The information in this chapter is presented in various formats so that the student will become more comfortable with the concept of test taking. Therefore, the authors have designed the activities in this chapter to provide the individual student with the tools necessary to be more successful on any future achievement tests. Working successfully through these exercises will improve the student's sense of pride and confidence in all areas of study. Fill in the circle next to the best answer.

MAKING USE OF MATHEMATICAL CONCEPTS

ACTIVITY: Read the following problems. There are four answers given for each question. You are to select the answer that you think is better than any of the others. Fill in the circle next to the best answer.

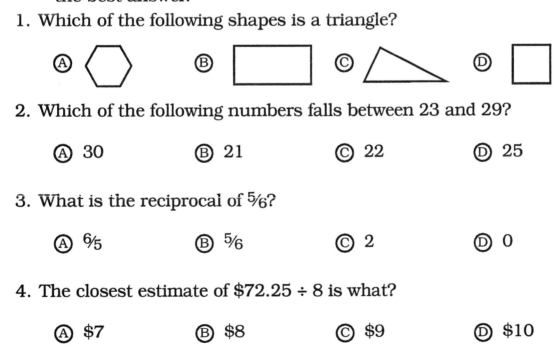

1. Which of the following shapes is a triangle?

   Ⓐ   Ⓑ   Ⓒ   Ⓓ

2. Which of the following numbers falls between 23 and 29?

  Ⓐ 30   Ⓑ 21   Ⓒ 22   Ⓓ 25

3. What is the reciprocal of $5/6$?

  Ⓐ $6/5$ Ⓑ $5/6$ Ⓒ 2   Ⓓ 0

4. The closest estimate of $72.25 ÷ 8 is what?

  Ⓐ $7   Ⓑ $8   Ⓒ $9   Ⓓ $10

STOP

SOLVING PROBLEMS USING BASIC MATH CONCEPTS

ACTIVITY: Read the following problems, and then fill in the circle of the best answer for each one.

1. Which following set of numbers has the greatest range?
   - (A) 22, 24, 27, 29
   - (B) ½, ⅚, 1¼, 3
   - (C) 4, 7, 8, 12
   - (D) 101, 103, 105, 107

2. If there are 36 eggs in 3 dozen, approximately how many eggs are there in 9 dozen?
   - (A) 72
   - (B) 110
   - (C) 95
   - (D) 125

3. What replaces the ? in the following number sentence?
   $$36 \times 6 = 4 \times (? + 4)$$
   - (A) 40
   - (B) 54
   - (C) 36
   - (D) 50

4. In the following shape, which figure is in a plane parallel to the plane containing DEF?

   - (A) ABC
   - (B) FAB
   - (C) DBA
   - (D) ABD

5. On the number line scale below, what number is missing as represented by the X?

   - (A) 3
   - (B) – 3
   - (C) – 4
   - (D) – 1

6. In the following sequence, which number would come next?
   $$1, 4, 16, 64, \underline{\quad ? \quad}$$
   - (A) 128
   - (B) 68
   - (C) 252
   - (D) 256

7. Which numeral below makes the number sentence true? $? < -9$
   - (A) – 8
   - (B) 8
   - (C) – 10
   - (D) 11

8. Of the following numbers, which one gives the prime factors of 243?
   - (A) $3 \times 9 \times 9$
   - (B) $3 \times 3 \times 3 \times 3 \times 3$
   - (C) $3 \times 3 \times 27$
   - (D) 3×81

STOP

SOLVING PROBLEMS USING BASIC MATH CONCEPTS

ACTIVITY: Read the following problems, and then fill in the circle of the best answer for each one.

1. What is another way to write 2 x 2 x 2 x 2 x 2?
   - Ⓐ 2 x 16
   - Ⓑ 2^5
   - Ⓒ 2 x 5
   - Ⓓ 10

2. On the following graph, what point is located at X = 2 and Y = 4?

   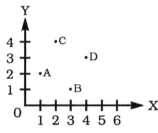

   - Ⓐ A
   - Ⓑ B
   - Ⓒ C
   - Ⓓ D

3. What is the closest estimate of 231 + 65?
   - Ⓐ 300
   - Ⓑ 200
   - Ⓒ 400
   - Ⓓ 100

4. If baking potatoes sell for $.49 a pound, about how much would 3½ pounds cost?
   - Ⓐ $1.50
   - Ⓑ $1.25
   - Ⓒ $.92
   - Ⓓ $1.75

5. What is the closest estimate of 7.24 ÷ 2.08?
   - Ⓐ 2.5
   - Ⓑ 3.5
   - Ⓒ 4.0
   - Ⓓ 3.0

6. What is the closest estimate of 4231 − 325?
   - Ⓐ 3900
   - Ⓑ 4000
   - Ⓒ 3800
   - Ⓓ 4200

7. What is the closest estimate of 38 + 56 + 49 + 83?
   - Ⓐ 220
   - Ⓑ 210
   - Ⓒ 230
   - Ⓓ 240

8. What is the closest estimate of 2¾ + 6½ + 7⅛?
   - Ⓐ 16
   - Ⓑ 18
   - Ⓒ 15
   - Ⓓ 17

9. If jeans are on sale for 50% off the regular price of $49.95, about how much would 3 pairs cost?
   - Ⓐ $75.00
   - Ⓑ $150.00
   - Ⓒ $100.00
   - Ⓓ $125.00

STOP

SOLVING GEOMETRIC AND NUMBER PROBLEMS

ACTIVITY: Read the following problems, and then fill in the circle next to the best answer for each one.

1. What is the volume of the six-sided rectangular solid below?

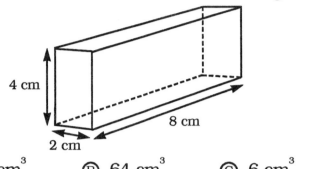

4 cm

8 cm

2 cm

Ⓐ 14 cm^3 Ⓑ 64 cm^3 Ⓒ 6 cm^3 Ⓓ 10 cm^3

2. What is the ratio of the area of Rectangle A to Rectangle B?

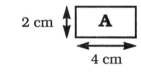

2 cm | **A**
4 cm

3 cm | **B**
8 cm

Ⓐ 3 to 1   Ⓑ 1 to 2   Ⓒ 1 to 3   Ⓓ 1 to 4

3. The average of three numbers is 6. Two of the numbers are 5 and 3. What is the other number?

Ⓐ 9   Ⓑ 6   Ⓒ 8   Ⓓ 10

4. Study the following angles. Of the angles, which one is congruent to angle R?

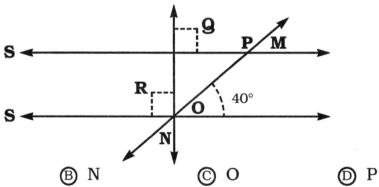

Ⓐ Q   Ⓑ N   Ⓒ O   Ⓓ P

5. What is another way to write 3^4?

Ⓐ 3 + 3 + 3 + 3   Ⓒ 3 x 3 x 3 x 3
Ⓑ 3 + 4   Ⓓ 3 x 4

STOP

APPLYING MATHEMATICAL CONCEPTS AND GRAPH INTERPRETATION

ACTIVITY: Read the following problems, and then fill in the circle of the correct answer to each one.

1. Which one of the following decimals is equal to ⅛?

   Ⓐ 12.5   Ⓑ .125   Ⓒ 1.25   Ⓓ .0125

2. What is another way to write 1.5 billion?

   Ⓐ 1,500,000   Ⓒ 1,500,000,000

   Ⓑ 15,000,000   Ⓓ 1,500,000,000,000

ACTIVITY: Study the following graph showing the enrollment in one school of seventh and eighth graders between 1990 and 1996. Then answer the questions that follow by filling in the circle of the best answer.

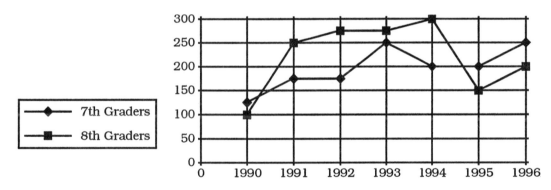

3. What was the total enrollment of seventh and eighth graders in 1994?

   Ⓐ 525   Ⓑ 350   Ⓒ 475   Ⓓ 500

4. How many eighth graders were enrolled in school in 1991?

   Ⓐ 100   Ⓑ 275   Ⓒ 250   Ⓓ 300

5. In which year was the enrollment of seventh graders greater than the eighth graders?

   Ⓐ 1994   Ⓑ 1995   Ⓒ 1992   Ⓓ 1991

6. What was the total enrollment of seventh and eighth grades in 1992, 1993, and 1994?

   Ⓐ 1450   Ⓑ 1475   Ⓒ 1400   Ⓓ 1375

STOP

MORE BASIC MATH APPLICATIONS

ACTIVITY: Read the following problems. For each question, fill in the circle next to the best answer.

1. In the following circle, what percent is shaded?

   Ⓐ 25%   Ⓑ 10%   Ⓒ 12½%   Ⓓ 16⅗%

2. Ladonna and Twyna are planning a biking picnic. They are taking sandwiches, cookies, chips, and soft drinks. Ladonna's lunch pack weighs 3½ pounds, and Twyna's pack weighs 2¼ pounds. How many ounces does Ladonna need to give Twyna to make both packs equal?

   Ⓐ 12   Ⓑ 10   Ⓒ 8   Ⓓ 14

3. If Jorge deposits $300 in a local bank account that pays 8% interest per year, how much interest will he earn in 1 year?

   Ⓐ $900.00   Ⓑ $24.00   Ⓒ $48.00   Ⓓ $72.00

4. Christy has a swimming pool that holds 30 kiloliters of water. If it takes her 5 minutes to add 10 kiloliters to the pool, how many minutes would it take to fill a 35 kiloliter pool?

   Ⓐ 17½   Ⓑ 15   Ⓒ 12½   Ⓓ 20

5. If you wanted to subtract 6 lb. 8 oz. from 8 lb. 5 oz., you would first convert 8 lb. 5 oz. to what?

   Ⓐ 8 lb. 13 oz.   Ⓑ 7 lb. 5 oz.   Ⓒ 7 lb. 21 oz.   Ⓓ 8 lb. 16 oz

6. If 8 hamburgers cost $3.39, about how much would 10 hamburgers cost?

   Ⓐ $4.00   Ⓑ $4.25   Ⓒ $4.50   Ⓓ $4.75

7. Thomas has 2 ten-dollar bills, 2 one-dollar bills, 3 dimes, 2 nickels, and 4 pennies. Cheri wants to borrow $3.49. How much will Thomas have if he loans her the money?

   Ⓐ $18.05   Ⓑ $18.90   Ⓒ $18.95   Ⓓ $25.93

STOP

SOLVING PROBLEMS USING BASIC MATH CONCEPTS

ACTIVITY: Read and study the following problems. For each question, fill in the circle of the best answer.

1. The Spanish Club had a fund-raising campaign during the month of October and made a profit of $425.00. The club collected $1,375.00 in sales. Approximately what percentage of the total amount collected was the profit?

   Ⓐ 3%   Ⓑ 300%   Ⓒ 30%   Ⓓ 36%

2. Study the following ruler measurement. Then decide what is the length from X to Z.

   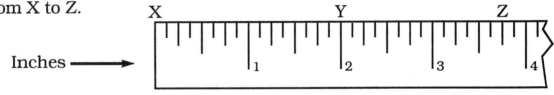

   Ⓐ 3⅜ inches   Ⓑ 2⅞ inches   Ⓒ 3½ inches   Ⓓ 3⅝ inches

3. In the following groups of numbers (or integers), which group is in order from greatest to least?

   Ⓐ 0, –1, 8, –4, 5, –8   Ⓒ –8, –7, –6, 0, 5, 8
   Ⓑ 8, 5, 0, –6, –7, –8   Ⓓ 8, 5, 0, –8, –6, –7

4. Heather read half of a novel on Tuesday. On Wednesday she read only 56 pages more. On Saturday she finished reading the book which had a total of 378 pages. By the end of Wednesday, how many pages had Heather read?

   Ⓐ 245   Ⓑ 189   Ⓒ 225   Ⓓ 212

5. What would replace the ? in the following equation? $\dfrac{12}{?} \times \dfrac{3}{6} = \dfrac{36}{78}$

   Ⓐ 12   Ⓑ 9   Ⓒ 14   Ⓓ 13

6. What is the mean of the following numbers?   8, 12, 4, 6, 3, 14, 2

   Ⓐ 11   Ⓑ 6   Ⓒ 7   Ⓓ 8

7. If you multiply 42 x 5000, how many zeros will the product have?

   Ⓐ 1   Ⓑ 3   Ⓒ 4   Ⓓ 2

STOP

SOLVING PROBLEMS USING BASIC MATH CONCEPTS

ACTIVITY: Read the following problems. For each question, fill in the circle of the best answer.

1. Which of the following numerals is the same as $^{16}\!/_{24}$?

    Ⓐ ¾   Ⓑ ⅝   Ⓒ ⅔   Ⓓ ⅜

2. What is a − b, if b + 200 = a?

    Ⓐ b + 200   Ⓑ 200   Ⓒ a + 200   Ⓓ 200 − b

3. What is the closest estimate of 5.31 x 3.48?

    Ⓐ 18   Ⓑ 19   Ⓒ 17   Ⓓ 20

4. Study the following two rectangles. The ratio of the area of rectangle X to rectangle Y is what?

    3 cm | **X** | 4 cm | **Y**
    4 cm   6 cm

    Ⓐ 2 to 1   Ⓑ 1 to 3   Ⓒ 1 to 4   Ⓓ 1 to 2

5. The closest estimate of 2.87 ÷ 14.35 is what?

    Ⓐ 20   Ⓑ 2   Ⓒ 20   Ⓓ 0.2

6. If a six-pack of cokes costs $3.29, then about how much would one coke cost?

    Ⓐ 53¢   Ⓑ 50¢   Ⓒ 56¢   Ⓓ 55¢

7. What is the closest estimate of 6.32 x .078?

    Ⓐ .49   Ⓑ 5   Ⓒ 4   Ⓓ 50

8. What is another way to write ⅓?

    Ⓐ .33   Ⓑ .25   Ⓒ .4   Ⓓ .16

9. According to Anthony's house plans, his bedroom is going to be 16 feet long. If 1 inch equals 2.5 feet, how long is his bedroom on the plan?

    Ⓐ 6 inches   Ⓑ 13.5 inches   Ⓒ 6.4 inches   Ⓓ 7 inches

STOP

MORE BASIC MATH PROBLEMS

ACTIVITY: Read the following problems. For each question, fill in the circle of the best answer.

1. How would one write *fifty-six and thirty-nine thousandths* in numbers?
   Ⓐ 0.56039   Ⓑ 0.5639   Ⓒ 56.039   Ⓓ 56,039.00

2. Study the following line points. Then decide which point shows the value of 3 + (2 − 5).

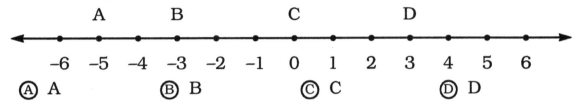

   A   B   C   D

  −6 −5 −4 −3 −2 −1 0 1 2 3 4 5 6

   Ⓐ A   Ⓑ B   Ⓒ C   Ⓓ D

3. If X = 10 and Y = 6, then which of the following equations would be true?
   Ⓐ X + Y = 4   Ⓒ X − Y = 6
   Ⓑ X − Y = 4   Ⓓ X − Y = 10

4. What is the closest estimate of $1\frac{1}{4} \div \frac{6}{8}$?
   Ⓐ 2   Ⓑ 1   Ⓒ 4   Ⓓ 3

5. Rounding to the nearest whole numbers, choose the estimate for the numbers 5.6 and 7.3.
   Ⓐ 5 and 7   Ⓑ 6 and 8   Ⓒ 5 and 8   Ⓓ 6 and 7

6. What is the greatest common factor of 18, 54, 90?
   Ⓐ 9   Ⓑ 3   Ⓒ 18   Ⓓ 6

7. Keith has 48 red marbles and 64 black marbles in a bucket. If he chooses one marble from the bucket, the odds are what in favor of choosing a red one?
   Ⓐ 4 to 3   Ⓑ 3 to 7   Ⓒ 1 to 8   Ⓓ 1 to 2

8. The following diagram shows the number of students who attended only football games, the number who attended only basketball games, and the number who attended both football *and* basketball games. How many students attended the basketball games?

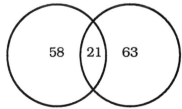

Football   Basketball

   Ⓐ 63   Ⓑ 84   Ⓒ 42   Ⓓ 85

STOP

SOLVING WORD PROBLEMS AND IMPROVING ESTIMATION SKILLS

ACTIVITY: Read the following problems. For each question, fill in the circle of the best answer.

1. Look at the following two squares A and B. If the sides of square A are twice as long as the sides of square B, then how many times greater is the area of square A than the area of square B?

   A | B

   Ⓐ 3 times greater   Ⓒ 4 times greater
   Ⓑ 2 times greater   Ⓓ 5 times greater

2. Mrs. Bailey bought 6 videotapes. The store sells packs of 2 videotapes for $6.32 and packs of 3 videotapes for $8.75. She bought the packs of 3. How much money did she save by not buying the packs of 2?

   Ⓐ $1.46   Ⓑ $2.46   Ⓒ 46¢   Ⓓ $1.06

3. The Spirit Club has 30 members. Each member plans to make 18 ribbons for the homecoming dance. However, 14 additional ribbons will have to be made. How many ribbons in all are needed for the dance?

   Ⓐ 540   Ⓑ 550   Ⓒ 564   Ⓓ 554

4. The closest estimate of $\frac{1}{2} + \frac{5}{8} + 1\frac{3}{16}$ is what?

   Ⓐ 3   Ⓑ 2   Ⓒ 1   Ⓓ 4

5. What is the closest estimate of 2132 x 6?

   Ⓐ 12,700   Ⓑ 12,900   Ⓒ 12,800   Ⓓ 1,280

6. The closest estimate of $61.93 – $49.96 is what?

   Ⓐ $11.00   Ⓑ $10.00   Ⓒ $2.00   Ⓓ $12.00

7. What is the closest estimate of 78.3 ÷ 9.25?

   Ⓐ 8   Ⓑ 9   Ⓒ 10   Ⓓ 7

8. The closest estimate of 297 x 200 is what?

   Ⓐ 60,000   Ⓑ 59,000   Ⓒ 49,000   Ⓓ 50,000

STOP

CHAPTER EIGHT:

IMPROVING MATH PROBLEM SOLVING, INTERPRETATION, AND COMPUTATION

Recognizing and understanding the relationships that exist among numbers are important skills to know in our rapidly changing technological world. These skills are not difficult to learn; however, you must know them, especially if you are going to be using fractions, percentages, money, tables, and graphs. The exercises presented in this chapter are developed to help you become a better student in such areas as addition, subtraction, multiplication, division, fractions, decimals, money, and problem solving. If you learn these skills now, your achievement scores in mathematics will improve and you will feel better about yourself.

ACTIVITY: Read the following problems. Fill in the circle of the correct answer. If the answer is not given, fill in the answer space marked **N.**

1. $\begin{array}{r} 832 \\ -\ 749 \end{array}$ Ⓐ 93   Ⓑ 193   Ⓒ 83   Ⓓ N

2. $1\frac{1}{2} - \frac{7}{8} =$ Ⓐ $\frac{5}{8}$ Ⓑ $\frac{3}{4}$ Ⓒ $1\frac{1}{4}$ Ⓓ N

3. $\begin{array}{r} 2383 \\ +\ 298 \end{array}$ Ⓐ 2682   Ⓑ 2680   Ⓒ 2581   Ⓓ N

4. $1\frac{1}{2} \times 12 =$ Ⓐ 18   Ⓑ 30   Ⓒ 6   Ⓓ N

5. $674 \div 37 =$ Ⓐ 18.29   Ⓑ 1.821   Ⓒ 18.22   Ⓓ N

6. $345 \times 31 =$ Ⓐ 10,035   Ⓑ 10,695   Ⓒ 9,365   Ⓓ N

STOP

WORKING NUMBER PROBLEMS

ACTIVITY: Read the following problems. For each question, fill in the circle of the correct answer. If the correct answer is not given, fill in the answer space marked N.

1. $3/8 \times 2/3 \times 1/2 =$ Ⓐ $7/48$ Ⓑ $6/13$ Ⓒ $1/8$ Ⓓ N

2. $15/7 \div 2\frac{1}{2} =$ Ⓐ $24/35$ Ⓑ $60/14$ Ⓒ $14/12$ Ⓓ N

3. $-60 \div -12 =$ Ⓐ -5   Ⓑ 5   Ⓒ 6   Ⓓ N

4.   31.02
   − 0.85   Ⓐ 30.17   Ⓑ 30.27   Ⓒ 31.17   Ⓓ N

5. $8 \times 3/4 =$ Ⓐ 5   Ⓑ 7   Ⓒ 4   Ⓓ N

6. $12 + (3 \times 13) =$ Ⓐ 41   Ⓑ 61   Ⓒ 51   Ⓓ N

7. $73.63 - 1.09 =$ Ⓐ 72.64   Ⓑ 72.54   Ⓒ 71.54   Ⓓ N

8. $12/14 + 5/7 =$ Ⓐ $1\,4/7$ Ⓑ $1\,5/7$ Ⓒ $23/14$ Ⓓ N

9. $\dfrac{9 + (36 \div 6)}{3} =$ Ⓐ 18   Ⓑ 17   Ⓒ 5   Ⓓ N

10. $6/8 + 3/9 =$ Ⓐ $1/4$ Ⓑ $1\,1/3$ Ⓒ $1\,1/12$ Ⓓ N

11. $638 \times 0.006 =$ Ⓐ 3.828   Ⓑ 38.28   Ⓒ .3828   Ⓓ N

12. $6.847 + 3.982 =$ Ⓐ 9.829   Ⓑ 10.829   Ⓒ 11.829   Ⓓ N

13. $538 \div 38 =$ Ⓐ 1.415   Ⓑ 141.51   Ⓒ 14.13   Ⓓ N

14. $3/5 \div 4/10 =$ Ⓐ $1\,1/2$ Ⓑ $1\,2/5$ Ⓒ $1\,9/20$ Ⓓ N

15. $72.8 \times 4.71 =$ Ⓐ 3428.888   Ⓑ 34.288   Ⓒ 342.888   Ⓓ N

16. $24 \div 2/4 =$ Ⓐ 12   Ⓑ 48   Ⓒ 24   Ⓓ N

17. $0.67 - 0.38 =$ Ⓐ 2.90   Ⓑ 0.029   Ⓒ 0.29   Ⓓ N

18. $4000 - 1058 =$ Ⓐ 3942   Ⓑ 1942   Ⓒ 2941   Ⓓ N

STOP

SOLVING WORD PROBLEMS AND INTERPRETING GRAPHS

ACTIVITY: Read the problems below. For each question, fill in the circle of the correct answer.

1. Shaun read 12 books, Vona read 8 books, and Amanda read 10 books. How can you figure out how many more books Shaun read than Amanda read?
   - (A) subtract 8 from 10
   - (B) add 8 and 10
   - (C) subtract 10 from 12
   - (D) subtract 8 from 12

2. Jill gave Courtney and Jarrad all her pennies. If Jill had 385 pennies and she gave Jarrad 4 times as many pennies as she gave Courtney, how many pennies did Courtney receive?
   - (A) 192
   - (B) 96
   - (C) 288
   - (D) 77

3. Sammy delivers daily newspapers, a total of 350 papers in 7 days. How many does he deliver each day?
   - (A) 35
   - (B) 46
   - (C) 50
   - (D) 55

ACTIVITY: Use the following chart to answer questions 4-6.

Favorite Birds of Students in Mrs. Hunt's Class

Redbird	/ / / / / /
Bluebird	/ / / / /
Dove	/ / / /
Hawk	/ / /
Wren	/ / / /

4. How many students are in Mrs. Hunt's class?
   - (A) 23
   - (B) 21
   - (C) 22
   - (D) Not Given

5. Which bird was the second most popular choice of students?
   - (A) Bluebird
   - (B) Redbird
   - (C) Wren
   - (D) Dove

6. Which fraction represents the number of students who chose the redbird?
   - (A) $3/11$
   - (B) $6/22$
   - (C) $7/22$
   - (D) $2/11$

STOP

SOLVING PROBLEMS USING GRAPH SKILLS

ACTIVITY: Read the following graph, and then answer the questions that follow by filling in the circle of the correct answer for each problem.

SPORTS ACTIVITIES OF 7TH AND 8TH GRADERS

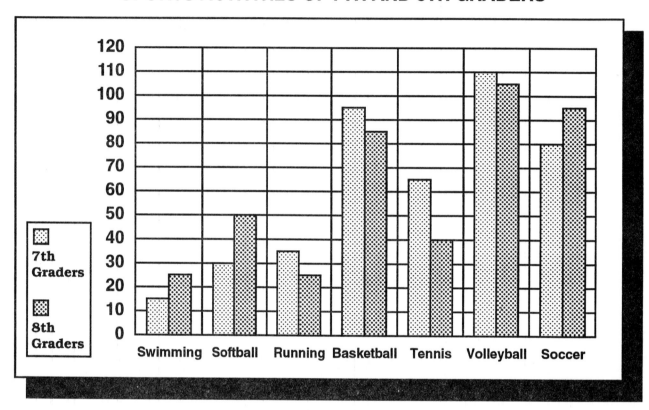

1. What is the difference between the number of seventh-grade swimming students and eighth-grade volleyball students?
   Ⓐ 80   Ⓑ 45   Ⓒ 90   Ⓓ 75

2. Which one of the following statements is true?
   Ⓐ The number of seventh-grade running students equals the number of eighth-grade tennis students.
   Ⓑ The difference between seventh-grade soccer students and eighth-grade basketball students is 5.
   Ⓒ The total number of volleyball students and tennis students is 330.
   Ⓓ The difference between the swimming students and softball students is 50.

3. What is the total number of students participating in swimming, running, tennis, and volleyball?
   Ⓐ 400   Ⓑ 410   Ⓒ 420   Ⓓ 430

STOP

SOLVING MATH WORD PROBLEMS

ACTIVITY: Read the following word problems. There are at least four answers given for each problem. Choose the answer that you think is better than any of the others, and then fill in the circle of the best answer for each question.

1. The seventh grade is having a picnic. Each student is inviting one person. There are 58 seventh graders. The teacher is coming, along with his guest. One fourth of the eighth grade class is coming to entertain the seventh graders. There are 56 eighth graders at school. How many people will be attending the picnic?

   Ⓐ 114   Ⓑ 122   Ⓒ 132   Ⓓ 144

2. If the school's total population is 3½ times the number of people going to the picnic, how many students are in the school?

   Ⓐ 462   Ⓑ 396   Ⓒ 452   Ⓓ 442

3. If each person attending the picnic eats one sandwich and the sandwiches are packaged in groups of 11 for $12.25, how much money is needed for everyone to have at least one sandwich?

   Ⓐ $146.50   Ⓑ $1,470.00   Ⓒ $14.70   Ⓓ $147.00

4. If drinks are purchased in six packs of $2.59 and 9 bags of chips cost $1.59 each, how much money will it take to buy the drinks and chips for everyone, considering everyone will receive one drink?

   Ⓐ $56.98   Ⓑ $71.29   Ⓒ $61.29   Ⓓ $71.19

5. Kyle is an eighth grader who rides to school with Jenny, Gregory, and Eleanor. Jenny's mother drives them to school and picks them up in the afternoon. She charges Kyle, Gregory, and Eleanor 50¢ each day for the service. If Jenny's mother uses 9 gallons of gas a week at a pump price of $1.09 per gallon, is she losing money or making money by taking the students to school? (Assume school is 20 days per month.)

   Ⓐ losing 76¢ a month   Ⓒ making 76¢ a month
   Ⓑ making $9.24 a month   Ⓓ losing $9.24 a month

6. Jenny lives 15 minutes from school. Kyle lives 4 minutes from Jenny; Eleanor lives 3 minutes from Kyle; Gregory lives 3 minutes from Eleanor; Gregory lives 7 minutes from school. How long does it take for Jenny's mother to take everyone to school?

   Ⓐ 15 minutes   Ⓑ 32 minutes   Ⓒ 17 minutes   Ⓓ 16 minutes

STOP

SOLVING PROBLEMS USING GRAPHING SKILLS

ACTIVITY: Study the following graph, and then fill in the circle of the best answer for each question.

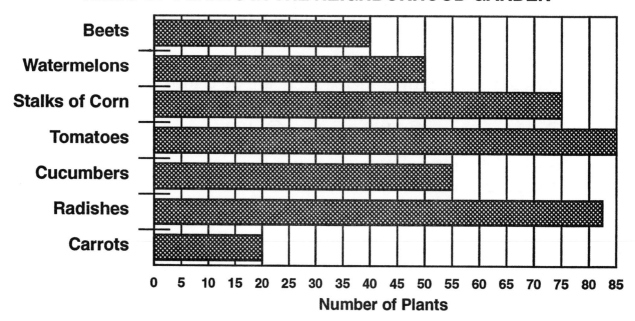

KINDS OF PLANTS IN THE NEIGHBORHOOD GARDEN

1. About how many radishes were produced?

   Ⓐ 75　　　　Ⓑ 77　　　　Ⓒ 80　　　　Ⓓ 82

2. Which produce yielded twice the amount of carrots?

   Ⓐ watermelons　　　　Ⓒ cucumbers
   Ⓑ beets　　　　　　　Ⓓ radishes

3. The yield of tomatoes was a little over two times that of which other produce?

   Ⓐ beets　　　　　　　Ⓒ radishes
   Ⓑ watermelons　　　　Ⓓ cucumbers

4. The neighborhood had a picnic and wanted to serve 168 people. All of the watermelons were cut equally, and each tossed salad contained at least 2 pieces of tomato cut equally. How many pieces of watermelon and tomato would be left over if each watermelon and tomato in the garden had been quartered?

   Ⓐ 2 watermelon, 2 tomato　　　　Ⓒ 32 watermelon, 4 tomato
   Ⓑ 3 watermelon, 6 tomato　　　　Ⓓ 24 watermelon, 2 tomato

STOP

SOLVING MATH WORD PROBLEMS

ACTIVITY: Read the following word problems. There are four answers given for each problem. Choose the answer that you think is better than any of the others, and then fill in the circle of the best answer for each question.

1. The volleyball team has a scheduled game at 7:00 P.M. The team must practice 2 hours before the game. It takes the team 15 minutes to dress, and the photographer wants to take a team picture which will take 15 minutes. What is the latest time the team can begin all these preparations?

   Ⓐ 3:30 P.M.   Ⓑ 5:30 P.M.   Ⓒ 4:45 P.M.   Ⓓ 4:30 P.M.

2. On the bus to the volleyball game were 12 seventh graders, 16 eighth graders, and 5 adults. How would you determine what percentage of the people on the bus were adults?

   Ⓐ subtract 5 from 33, then multiply by 100
   Ⓑ divide 5 by 33, then multiply by 100
   Ⓒ divide 5 by 33, then multiply by 10
   Ⓓ divide 33 by 5, then multiply by 10

3. If in question #2 one fourth of the seventh graders were girls and five eighths of the eighth graders were boys, how many female students were on the bus?

   Ⓐ 10   Ⓑ 13   Ⓒ 9   Ⓓ 16

4. Heather's mother gave her enough money to buy the 5 books for sale at the school bookstore. In fact, her mother expected some change back from the money she had given Heather. What do we have to know to figure out how much change her mother will receive?

   Ⓐ how much the books cost
   Ⓑ how much the books cost and how much money Heather's mother had given her
   Ⓒ how much lunch will cost
   Ⓓ how much the new math book costs

STOP

USING A CHART TO SOLVE WORD PROBLEMS

ACTIVITY: Study the following chart. For each question, fill in the circle of the best answer.

SPANISH CLUB RECORDS

MONTH	EXPENSES	INCOME
August	0.00	125.00
September	32.00	0.00
October	55.00	145.00
November	0.00	37.70
December	32.75	1,235.75
January	1,195.00	0.00
February	0.00	0.00
March	15.75	92.50
April	44.70	0.00
May	21.50	0.00
June	0.00	66.50
July	0.00	71.25

1. How much profit did the Spanish Club clear for the month of December?
   Ⓐ $1,235.75   Ⓑ $32.75   Ⓒ $1,203.00   Ⓓ $1,268.50

2. At the end of July, did the club have a profit or a loss for the year? How much was it?
   Ⓐ Loss, $377.00   Ⓒ Profit, $1,773.70
   Ⓑ Profit, $387.00   Ⓓ Profit, $377.00

3. For **March**, about what percent were the expenses compared to the income?
   Ⓐ 16%   Ⓑ 61%   Ⓒ 33%   Ⓓ 25%

4. **During which 2 months** did the expenses and profits almost balance each other?
   Ⓐ March and April   Ⓒ May and June
   Ⓑ December and January   Ⓓ October and November

5. What was the profit or loss for the months of December and January?
   Ⓐ Loss, $8.00   Ⓒ Profit, $8.00
   Ⓑ Profit, $28.00   Ⓓ Loss, $28.00

6. During which month is the difference between the expenses and the income the greatest?
   Ⓐ January   Ⓑ October   Ⓒ August   Ⓓ December

STOP

SOLVING MATH WORD PROBLEMS

ACTIVITY: Read the following word problems. There are four answers given for each problem. Choose the answer that you think is better than any others, and then fill in the circle of the best answer for each word problem.

1. Veronica and Diana joined a book club. For one month their total amount due was $36.00. Veronica's amount due was twice as much as Diana's. How much did Diana pay?

Ⓐ $9.00   Ⓑ $6.00   Ⓒ $24.00   Ⓓ $12.00

2. During December, Veronica ordered an $8.00 book reduced from $12.95, a $12.50 book reduced from $16.75, and a $22.25 book reduced from $31.65. Diana only ordered one that was reduced from $15.89 to $10.99. Approximately what percent of the total bill was Veronica's?

Ⓐ 25%   Ⓑ 75%   Ⓒ $33%   Ⓓ 66%

3. In the spring during a book sale, Diana ordered a three-volume set of books for $31.25 instead of paying $12.95 for each of the three books. By buying the set, about what percent did she save?

Ⓐ 25%   Ⓑ 80%   Ⓒ 20%   Ⓓ 75%

4. The book club adds 10% to the amount due to include shipping and handling costs. What would Veronica and Diana's total bill be for the month of June if Veronica ordered two books for $7.95 each, a book for $5.95, and a book for $11.95, and Diana ordered three books at $9.99 each?

Ⓐ $70.15   Ⓑ $66.37   Ⓒ $63.77   Ⓓ $69.14

5. During the month of August, the book club offered a back-to-school special. Veronica ordered two books that were $9.79 each minus a 25% discount and one book that was $5.95 minus 20%. Diana bought one book that was $14.95 minus 30%. How much money did they owe including the shipping costs?

Ⓐ $29.91   Ⓑ $31.82   Ⓒ $32.92   Ⓓ $29.92

STOP

INTERPRETING LINE GRAPHS

ACTIVITY: Study the following graph about Moore's Car City. This graph shows the number of cars sold during one year. Choose the best answer, and fill in the circle next to the correct answer for each question.

MOORE'S CAR CITY

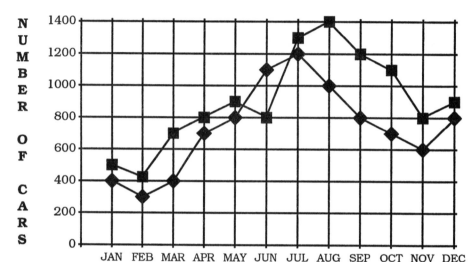

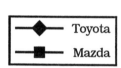

1. What is the closest estimate of the number of car sales for Toyota during January, February, March, and April?

   Ⓐ 1,100   Ⓑ 1,400   Ⓒ 1,600   Ⓓ 1,800

2. During which month did Mazda's sales slip lower than Toyota's sales?

   Ⓐ February   Ⓑ May   Ⓒ June   Ⓓ November

3. What is the closest estimate of the number of car sales for Mazda for September, October, November, and December?

   Ⓐ 2,100   Ⓑ 3,400   Ⓒ 2,600   Ⓓ 4,000

4. During which month did car sales reach their highest point?

   Ⓐ June   Ⓑ July   Ⓒ August   Ⓓ September

5. During which month did sales of both types of cars increase in volume?

   Ⓐ January   Ⓑ May   Ⓒ September   Ⓓ November

STOP

CHAPTER NINE:

INTERPRETING MAPS, CHARTS, AND DIAGRAMS

Learning to read maps, charts, and diagrams is an important everyday problem-solving skill. News reports, weather reports, current events, and travel, as well as many occupations, require the ability to read and to understand such illustrative tools. Gaining experience with maps, charts, and diagrams will help you develop basic skills needed in school and in life. Work through the activities with your parents or teachers in order to improve your everyday problem-solving abilities.

LEARNING TO READ CHARTS

ACTIVITY: Using the chart below, choose the best answer for each question. Fill in the circle before each correct answer.

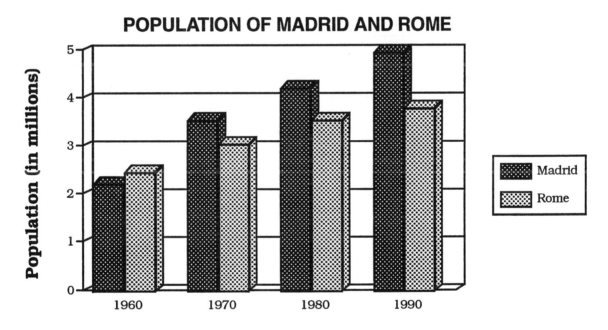

POPULATION OF MADRID AND ROME

1. The information on this graph covers a ____-year period.
   Ⓐ 10   Ⓑ 20   Ⓒ 30   Ⓓ 40

2. In which year did Rome have a larger population than Madrid?
   Ⓐ 1990   Ⓑ 1980   Ⓒ 1970   Ⓓ 1960

3. In which year was Rome's population nearly 4 million?
   Ⓐ 1990   Ⓑ 1980   Ⓒ 1970   Ⓓ 1960

4. In 1970 Madrid's population was approximately ____ million.
   Ⓐ 3   Ⓑ 3.5   Ⓒ 4   Ⓓ 4.5

STOP

USING A GRAPH

ACTIVITY: A graph is a diagram using dots, lines, bars, or circles to show relationships between things. Graphs are functional and are often used because they are more easily interpreted than a list of numbers. Much information can be shown on a graph. Below is a line graph comparing the U.S. rivers.

Answer the questions below after studying the graph. Fill in the circle next to each correct answer.

RIVERS OF THE UNITED STATES

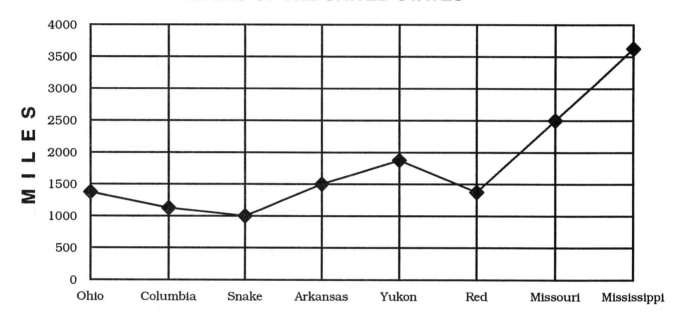

1. Based on the graph, about how long is the Yukon River?
   ① 800 miles   ② 1,400 miles   ③ 1,800 miles   ④ 600 miles

2. How much longer is the Missouri River than the Ohio River?
   ① 600 miles   ② 1,200 miles   ③ 1,000 miles   ④ 1,600 miles

3. According to the graph, what is the shortest river?
   ① Ohio River   ② Red River   ③ Snake River   ④ Yukon River

4. What is the third longest river according to the graph?
   ① Yukon   ② Arkansas   ③ Columbia   ④ Missouri

5. Judging from the graph, what is the longest river?
   ① Missouri   ② Arkansas   ③ Columbia   ④ Mississippi

STOP

LEARNING TO READ MAPS

ACTIVITY: Use the Vatican City map to answer the questions that follow. Fill in the circle next to the correct answer for each question.

1. What is located directly west of St. Peter's Square?
   - Ⓐ the Gardens
   - Ⓑ the Vatican Museums
   - Ⓒ the Papal Palace
   - Ⓓ St. Peter's Basilica

2. From north to south, Vatican City is approximately _____ in length at its greatest point.
   - Ⓐ 2,400 ft. (732 m)
   - Ⓑ 1,800 ft. (549 m)
   - Ⓒ 1,200 ft. (366 m)
   - Ⓓ 600 ft. (183 m)

3. Approximately how long are the Vatican Museums together, in feet?
   - Ⓐ 200 ft.
   - Ⓑ 600 ft.
   - Ⓒ 1,200 ft.
   - Ⓓ 1,400 ft.

4. St. Peter's Square is located near the _____ corner of Vatican City.
   - Ⓐ northwestern
   - Ⓑ southwestern
   - Ⓒ northeastern
   - Ⓓ southeastern

5. The Sistine Chapel is part of _____ .
   - Ⓐ the Vatican Museums
   - Ⓑ St. Peter's Basilica
   - Ⓒ St. Peter's Square
   - Ⓓ the Gardens

6. Vatican City, the independent state, is located within _____ .
   - Ⓐ Paris
   - Ⓑ London
   - Ⓒ Rome
   - Ⓓ New York

STOP

LEARNING TO READ MAPS

ACTIVITY: Use the map below of northern South America to answer the questions concerning climate. Fill in the circle before the correct answer for each question below.

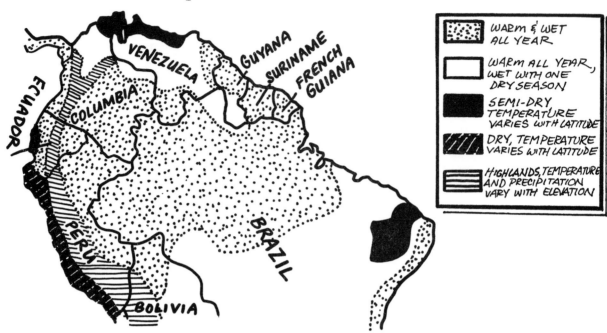

1. Most of the areas on this map have a climate that is usually _____ .
   ⓐ semi-dry with varying temperatures
   ⓑ cool all year
   ⓒ warm all year
   ⓓ dry with one wet season

2. How many climates are there in the country of Colombia?
   ⓐ one   ⓑ two   ⓒ three   ⓓ four

3. In which part of Brazil is the climate semi-dry?
   ⓐ northern   ⓑ southern   ⓒ eastern   ⓓ western

4. According to the map, temperature and precipitation vary with elevation in the highlands of Colombia and _____ .
   ⓐ Ecuador   ⓑ Brazil   ⓒ Suriname   ⓓ Guyana

5. Most of Venezuela is in which climate zone?
   ⓐ semi-dry, temperature varies
   ⓑ warm all year, wet with one dry season
   ⓒ warm and wet all year
   ⓓ cool all year

STOP

LEARNING TO READ MAPS

ACTIVITY: Use the map of eastern Asia to answer the questions concerning China and its neighbors. Fill in the circle before the correct answer for each question below.

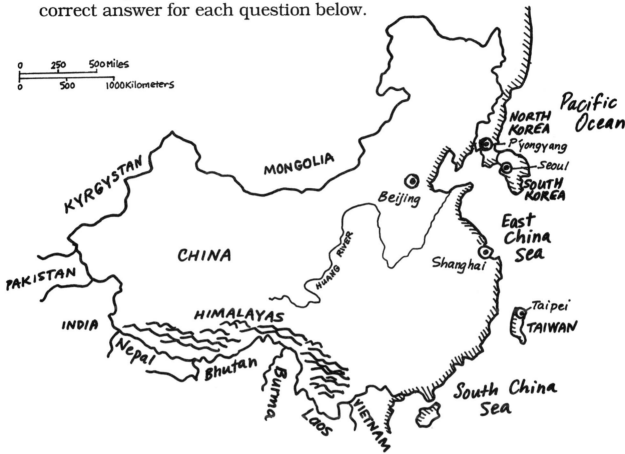

1. The Himalayas are a mountain range in which area of China?
   ⓐ north   ⓑ south   ⓒ east   ⓓ west

2. What body of water is south and east of China?
   ⓐ South China Sea   ⓒ Pacific Ocean
   ⓑ Huang River   ⓓ East China Sea

3. Which independent country is an island?
   ⓐ South Korea   ⓒ Macau
   ⓑ Vietnam   ⓓ Taiwan

4. At its longest point (north to south), what is China's approximate length in miles?
   ⓐ 1,500   ⓑ 1,800   ⓒ 2,500   ⓓ 3,200

5. What is the capital of North Korea?
   ⓐ Seoul   ⓑ Beijing   ⓒ Taipei   ⓓ P'yongyang

STOP

LEARNING TO READ MAPS

ACTIVITY: Using the map of Southeast Asia, answer the questions below the map. Fill in the circle before the correct answer for each question.

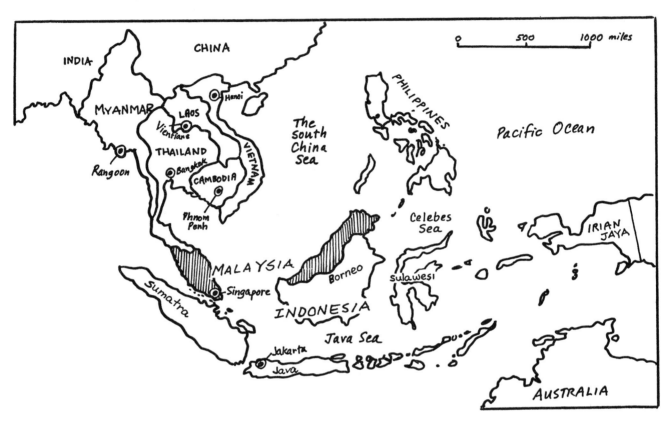

1. What body of water lies between Vietnam and the Philippines?
   - ⓐ the Celebes Sea
   - ⓑ the Andaman Sea
   - ⓒ the South China Sea
   - ⓓ the Pacific Ocean

2. Phnom Penh is the national capital of _____ .
   - ⓐ Cambodia
   - ⓑ Laos
   - ⓒ Thailand
   - ⓓ Myanmar

3. Singapore is located _____ of Cambodia.
   - ⓐ north
   - ⓑ south
   - ⓒ east
   - ⓓ west

4. What is the national capital of Thailand?
   - ⓐ Jakarta
   - ⓑ Vientiane
   - ⓒ Bangkok
   - ⓓ Hanoi

5. Java and Sumatra are two of the islands of _____ .
   - ⓐ Indonesia
   - ⓑ Australia
   - ⓒ the Philippines
   - ⓓ Malaysia

STOP

CHAPTER TEN:

APPLYING LIBRARY AND STUDY SKILLS

It is important to learn to use the library because there are so many valuable resources available that can help you in almost any kind of research. In the library are found such resources as dictionaries, atlases, almanacs, encyclopedias, magazines, newspapers, and many more. Using these resource materials properly will make learning more fun and help save time when doing research on particular projects. Furthermore, if you feel more comfortable using the library, then you will become more confident as a student.

ACQUIRING LIBRARY SKILLS

ACTIVITY: Read the following questions. Answer the questions by filling in the circle next to the best answer.

1. If you wanted to find the meaning of the word **pretentious,** you would probably use which source?
   - Ⓐ dictionary
   - Ⓑ encyclopedia
   - Ⓒ almanac
   - Ⓓ atlas

2. If you wanted to find a copy of "The Declaration of Independence," which source would you use?
   - Ⓐ dictionary
   - Ⓑ thesaurus
   - Ⓒ encyclopedia
   - Ⓓ biographical dictionary

3. If you wanted to find the average yearly rainfall in Madagascar, in which source would you look?
   - Ⓐ thesaurus
   - Ⓑ atlas
   - Ⓒ dictionary
   - Ⓓ biographical dictionary

4. If you wanted to find another word for **supernatural,** you would probably use which source?
   - Ⓐ dictionary
   - Ⓑ atlas
   - Ⓒ thesaurus
   - Ⓓ biographical dictionary

5. If you were collecting information on the current presidential election, which source would be the most helpful?
   - Ⓐ dictionary
   - Ⓑ magazine
   - Ⓒ encyclopedia
   - Ⓓ atlas

STOP

USING THE DEWEY DECIMAL SYSTEM

ACTIVITY: The Dewey Decimal System, which classifies nonfiction
books in ten major categories according to subject, was designed
by Melvil Dewey. He designed this system by assigning numbers
to designate general categories. This Dewey Decimal number, or
call number, simplifies book selection and organization in the
library. Use the categories below to answer the questions that
follow. Circle the correct answer to each question.

Numbers	*Category*
000 - 099	General Works (encyclopedias, magazines, newspapers)
100 - 199	Philosophy (psychology, ethics)
200 - 299	Religion (mythology, world religions)
300 - 399	Social Sciences (economics, government, law, education)
400 - 499	Languages (grammar, dictionaries)
500 - 599	Pure Sciences (math, astronomy, chemistry, physics, biology, botany, zoology)
600 - 699	Technology (medicine, engineering, business, gardening, home economics)
700 - 799	Arts (architecture, drawing, painting, music, sports, recreation)
800 - 899	Literature (plays, poetry, essays)
900 - 999	Geography and History (travel, biographies)

1. Where would the book *Rivers of Argentina* be found?
   - Ⓐ 100–199
   - Ⓑ 300–399
   - Ⓒ 700–799
   - Ⓓ 900–999

2. Where would you find a book about art history?
   - Ⓐ 000–099
   - Ⓑ 200–299
   - Ⓒ 700–799
   - Ⓓ 900–999

3. What subject area is dealt with books numbered in the 600s?
   - Ⓐ Technology
   - Ⓒ Religion, Myths
   - Ⓑ Literature (Plays & Poetry)
   - Ⓓ Pure Sciences

4. Where would the book *Studies in English Grammar* be found?
   - Ⓐ 300–399
   - Ⓑ 400–499
   - Ⓒ 700–799
   - Ⓓ 800–899

5. What subject is found in books numbered in the 500s?
   - Ⓐ Geography, History
   - Ⓒ Technology
   - Ⓑ Religion, Myths
   - Ⓓ Pure Sciences

STOP

USING REFERENCE MATERIALS

ACTIVITY: Read the following sample subject entry which would resemble one found in the *Readers' Guide to Periodical Literature,* a great resource in the library containing numerous topics and titles of magazines. Then circle the correct answer for each question.

Subject Entry

Smoking
    How Bad Is Smoking? *Science Weekly* 40: 395–399 S 6 '95
    Teenage Smokers B. F. Whiteside. il. *Science and Today* 103:
    48–51 Ag 8 '91
    Kick the Habit—and Live P. Barclift. il. *Living World*
    58: 76–78 Jl 21 '95
    Smoking at School—The Principals Say No! D. J. Ralph.
    il. *Middle School Times* 24: 15–19 My 5 '93
    Peer Pressure Goes up in Smoke M. Rungrunang il.
    High School Journal 15: 83–89 O '95

---

1. What is the name of the article written by D. J. Ralph?
   - Ⓐ "Peer Pressure Goes up in Smoke"
   - Ⓑ "Kick the Habit—and Live"
   - Ⓒ "Smoking at School—The Principals Say No!"
   - Ⓓ "Teenage Smokers"

2. On what pages would one find the article "Teenage Smokers"?
   - Ⓐ 83-89
   - Ⓑ 395-399
   - Ⓒ 15-19
   - Ⓓ 48-51

3. During which month did the article "Peer Pressure Goes up in Smoke" appear?
   - Ⓐ May
   - Ⓑ October
   - Ⓒ August
   - Ⓓ September

4. In which year did the article "Kick the Habit—and Live" appear?
   - Ⓐ 1991
   - Ⓑ 1993
   - Ⓒ 1995
   - Ⓓ 1994

5. Who wrote the article "How Bad Is Smoking"?
   - Ⓐ P. Barclift
   - Ⓒ *Science Weekly*
   - Ⓑ M. Rungrunang
   - Ⓓ Not Given

6. In which article would one find information about what school officials are doing concerning smoking at school?
   - Ⓐ "Peer Pressure Goes up in Smoke"
   - Ⓑ "Smoking at School—The Principals Say No!"
   - Ⓒ "Kick the Habit—and Live"
   - Ⓓ "How Bad Is Smoking?"

STOP

USING REFERENCE MATERIALS

ACTIVITY: Study the following sample printout which would closely resemble a printout from the *Automated Index to Periodical Literature*. After typing in the words *smoking*, then *teenagers*, then *school* on the *Automated Index*, a list of sources similar to the following would appear on the screen. Study the list carefully and then answer the questions that follow by filling in the circle before each correct answer.

---

7.   Teenagers — Tobacco — United States
To smoke or not to smoke. By Bates, John K.
(Teen Review, Nov95, Vol. 18 Issue 22, p58, 4p, 3c)
(0070–4100)
*** Full text available on CD-ROM ***
(We subscribe to this magazine.)

8.   Teenagers — Use of tobacco — United States
Cigarettes in school. By Johnson, Kevin C.
(The Principal's Quarterly, Oct95, Vol. 58 Issue 27,
p105, 5p, 6c) (1065–3045)
*** Full text available on CD-ROM ***
(We do not subscribe to this magazine.)

9.   Adolescents — Tobacco products — United States
What do parents think and do? By Benson, Heather A.
(Changes, 11/24/95, Vol. 43 Issue 31, p86, 8p, 3c)
(1065–2078)
*** Full text available on CD-ROM ***
(We subscribe to this magazine.)

---

1. Who wrote the article entitled "To Smoke or Not to Smoke"?
   - Ⓐ Heather Benson
   - Ⓑ Kevin Johnson
   - Ⓒ John Bates
   - Ⓓ Not Given

2. On what page can you find the article entitled "What Do Parents Think and Do?"
   - Ⓐ 31
   - Ⓑ 86
   - Ⓒ 43
   - Ⓓ 1065-2078

3. What is the name of the magazine article found in *The Principal's Quarterly*?
   - Ⓐ "Teenagers"
   - Ⓑ "To Smoke or Not to Smoke"
   - Ⓒ "Use of Tobacco"
   - Ⓓ "Cigarettes in School"

4. On what month and day did the article "What Do Parents Think and Do?" appear?
   - Ⓐ October 24
   - Ⓑ November 9
   - Ⓒ November 24
   - Ⓓ Not Given

5. Who is the author of "Cigarettes in School"?
   - Ⓐ Kevin Johnson
   - Ⓑ Heather Benson
   - Ⓒ John Bates
   - Ⓓ Not Given

STOP

ACTIVITY: Read and study the following index from *How to Write a Great Research Paper* (Incentive Publications, 1994. Used by permission.). Then answer the questions by filling in the circle of each correct answer.

INDEX

Almanacs, 20–21

Atlases, 20

Automated Card Catalog, 24

Card Catalog, 14–15

CD–ROM, 24

Computers and the Library, 24–26

Dictionaries, 20

Final Paper, 71–82

Footnotes, 45, 47

On–Line Network, 25

Outlines
Final Outlines, 57–62
Preliminary Outlines, 37–44
See Final Paper

Plagiarism, 34

Resources and Materials, 19–26

Student Samples
Bibliography, 69
Final draft, 72–82
First draft, 51–53
Thesis statement, 38

Virtual Reality, 25

1. On which page(s) would you look to find information on the electronic highway?
Ⓐ 24 Ⓑ 20–21 Ⓒ 24–26 Ⓓ 19–26

2. If you wanted to look at a completed research paper, one that was ready to be submitted, on which page(s) would you probably look?
Ⓐ 51–53 Ⓑ 69 Ⓒ 71–82 Ⓓ 38

3. On which page(s) would you look to find information on copying without giving credit to the source(s) from which you copied?
Ⓐ 19–26 Ⓑ 25 Ⓒ 20 Ⓓ 34

4. If you were interested in learning more about the card catalog on computer, on what page(s) would you look?
Ⓐ 24 Ⓑ 14–15 Ⓒ 25 Ⓓ 23

5. Which page(s) would probably give you information on doing your first outline?
Ⓐ 57–62 Ⓒ 72–82
Ⓑ 37–44 Ⓓ 51–53

6. If you wanted to know more about the reference material which contains maps of countries in the world, on which page(s) would you look?
Ⓐ 25 Ⓑ 24–26 Ⓒ 20 Ⓓ 21

STOP

USING THE DICTIONARY

ACTIVITY: Using this partial dictionary entry, answer questions 1–7 by circling the best answer for each question.

1. Which is the correct spelling of the word meaning "to make known to a general mass of people"?
   - (A) pouluarize
   - (B) popularize
   - (C) popalurize
   - (D) popularise

2. Which word fits best in the sentence "Elvis was a _____ musical performer"?
   - (A) poplar
   - (B) populist
   - (C) popular
   - (D) pop-top

3. Which entry word comes immediately before **population?**
   - (A) popularize
   - (B) populating
   - (C) populist
   - (D) populate

4. Which word fits in the sentence "The fancy mansion had a large collection of _____ vases"?
   - (A) porcelain
   - (B) populous
   - (C) Popsicle
   - (D) poplin

5. What is the correct spelling of the word meaning "fast-growing tree having triangular leaves"?
   - (A) poplin
   - (B) popllar
   - (C) poplar
   - (D) popular

6. What is the plural of poppy?
   - (A) poppies
   - (B) popies
   - (C) poppys
   - (D) poppyies

7. Which sentence uses the word **populist** correctly?
   - (A) What is the current *populist* of your city?
   - (B) He is the *populist* person in the eighth grade.
   - (C) The flower of the poppy plant is called a *populist*.
   - (D) In the past Americans have had the choice of voting for a candidate from the *populist* party.

---

poplar / porcelain

pop•lar (pŏp′lər) *n.* Fast-growing tree having triangular leaves and soft light-colored wood.

pop•lin (pŏp′lĭn) *n.* A fabric of rayon, silk, wool, or cotton with fine crosswise ridges, used in making clothing.

pop•o•ver (pŏp′ō′vər) *n.* A light muffin which expands during baking and "pops over" the perimeter of the pan.

pop•pa (pä′pə) *n.* Another form of papa.

pop•py (pŏp′ē) *n., pl.* poppies. Plant with ornamental, frequently bright-red flowers.

poppy

pop•py•cock (pŏp′ē kŏk′) *n.* Nonsensical talk; foolish comments (not used formally).

Pop•si•cle (pŏp′sĭ kəl) *n.* Flavored, colored ice with a sweet taste that is held by a handle of one or two sticks. (A trademark name)

pop-top (pŏp′tŏp′) *adj.* Description of a container with a tab that can be removed to produce an opening, e.g. soft drink can.

pop•u•lace (pŏp′yə lĭs) *n.* The mass of people.

pop•u•lar (pŏp′yə lər) *adj.* Accepted or liked by many people.

pop•u•lar•i•ty (pŏp′yə lăr′ĭ tē) *n.* A position of being well-liked by the majority of people.

pop•u•lar•ize (pŏp′yələ rīz′) *v.* To make known to a general mass of people.

pop•u•lar•ly (pŏp′yə lər lē) *adv.* Usually; generally.

pop•u•late (pŏp′yə lāt′) *v.* To inhabit an area.

pop•u•la•tion (pŏp′yə lā′shən) *n.* The total number of people, animals, or plants in a region.

pop•u•list (pŏp′yəlĭst) *n.* Someone who supports and promotes rights of the common, ordinary person.

pop•u•lous (pŏp′yələs) *adj.* Thickly populated.

por•ce•lain (pôr′səlĭn) *n.* A hard white material formed by heating a type of clay at a high temperature and then coating it with many different-colored materials.

Abbreviations: *n.* = noun; *adj.* = adjective; *v.* = verb; *adv.* = adverb.

STOP

ACTIVITY: Study the following Table of Contents from *Composition and Creative Writing for Middle Grades* (Incentive Publications, 1991), and then circle the correct answer to each question.

TABLE OF CONTENTS

---

1. Suppose you have just completed reading a short story and your teacher asks you to tell or write the story in your own words. In which chapter would you probably find information on learning how to tell or write something in your own words?
   - Ⓐ UFOs
   - Ⓑ Meal Appeal
   - Ⓒ Paraphrase Crazy
   - Ⓓ The Boa That Burst

2. Heronda's teacher said that Heronda was smart as a whip. If you wanted to find other expressions similar to "smart as a whip," in which chapter would you look?
   - Ⓐ The Word Co-Op
   - Ⓑ Jukebox Jargon
   - Ⓒ Catch A Cliché
   - Ⓓ Play On Words

3. André's father is a dentist. Occasionally his father jokes that his "occupation is very filling." In which chapter would you look to find other similar expressions?
   - Ⓐ As Smart As A Whip
   - Ⓑ Private Eye
   - Ⓒ Sail A Story
   - Ⓓ Pun Fun

4. Levente's teacher has been encouraging him to expand his imagery in his writing by creating more direct comparisons. One example he gave Levente was "And she walked along the sandy beach like Venus in the clouds." In which chapter would Levente look to find more examples of these comparisons?
   - Ⓐ As Smart As A Whip
   - Ⓑ The Word Co-Op
   - Ⓒ Pun Fun
   - Ⓓ Jukebox Jargon

STOP

USING OUTLINES

ACTIVITY: Read and study the following outline by Tonya Collins on the Bermuda Triangle, and then answer the questions that follow by filling in the circle next to the correct answer to each one.

THE BERMUDA TRIANGLE

I. Introduction
   A. _____
   B. No calls for help

II. Legend
   A. Military craft
   B. Christmas winds
   C. U.S.S. Cyclops

III. _____
   A. Flying saucer
   B. Disintegration
   C. _____
   D. Atmospheric disturbance
   E. Gravitational disturbance
   F. Electromagnetic disturbance

IV. Conclusion

---

1. There is a blank at main topic III. Which one of the following would be most appropriate?
   Ⓐ Discoveries
   Ⓑ Truths
   Ⓒ Areas
   Ⓓ Explanations

2. If you were researching the likelihood of interruptions or commotions in the air above the Bermuda Triangle, then you would want to read particularly what part of the outline in the paper?
   Ⓐ II-A   Ⓒ III-A
   Ⓑ III-D   Ⓓ I-B

3. Which one of the following is most likely the best topic for III-C?
   Ⓐ Media events
   Ⓑ Facts
   Ⓒ Natural force
   Ⓓ U.S.S. America

4. If you wanted to know if any planes or ships had crashed or sunk in the Bermuda Triangle, you would find this information in which part of the outline?
   Ⓐ II-A   Ⓒ II-B
   Ⓑ III-A   Ⓓ IV

5. If the beginning of this paper is about all the publicity which the Bermuda Triangle has received in the past few years, then which of the following subtopics would be most appropriate for I-A?
   Ⓐ Television and the Bermuda Triangle
   Ⓑ Newspaper and radio coverage
   Ⓒ President's address to the nation
   Ⓓ Media events

STOP

ANSWER KEY

Page 16
1. get back
2. main idea
3. bad-tempered
4. go up and down

Page 17
1. B
2. D
3. C
4. A
5. D
6. B
7. A
8. C
9. D
10. A

Page 18
11. C
12. B
13. D
14. B
15. A
16. C
17. D
18. A
19. C
20. B

Page 19
1. ①
2. ②
3. ④
4. ①
5. ③
6. ①
7. ④
8. ②
9. ③
10. ②

Page 20
1. cents
2. through
3. heir
4. too
5. your
6. right, write
7. four
8. sealing
9. It's
10. patients, patience

11. principals, principles
12. or
13. week, weak
14. their
15. weight, wait
16. altar, alter

Page 21
1. C
2. B
3. D
4. C
5. A
6. D
7. A
8. B

Page 22
1. A
2. C
3. D
4. B

Page 23
1. B
2. D
3. A
4. B
5. C

Page 24
1. C
2. D
3. A
4. C
5. B
6. D
7. C
8. C
9. A
10. D

Page 25
1. d
2. a
3. d
4. c

Page 26
A. ⑤
B. ③

C. ③
D. ①
E. ②
F. ⑤
G. ③
H. ③
I. ①
J. ③
K. ②
L. ③

Page 27
M. ①
N. ⑤
O. ③
P. ①
Q. ②
R. ③
S. ①
T. ③
U. ①
V. ⑤
W. ①
X. ③

Page 28
1. a, climate
2. d, yacht
3. d, puzzle
4. b, familiar
5. c, magazine
6. b, besieged
7. b, silhouette
8. d, distinguish
9. a, windshield
10. c, disobedient
11. a, distress
12. d, defective
13. a, oblige

Page 29
1. A
2. D
3. B
4. C
5. A
6. D
7. B
8. A
9. C
10. B

Page 30
11. B
12. D
13. A
14. C
15. D
16. A
17. B
18. C
19. C
20. D
21. A
22. C

Page 31
1. C
2. C
3. B
4. A
5. B
6. D
7. B
8. B
9. C
10. A

Page 32
1. B
2. C
3. A

Page 34
1. D
2. B
3. C
4. A
5. C
6. C
7. A

Page 35
1. B
2. D
3. C
4. B

Page 37
1. C
2. D
3. A
4. B
5. B
6. C

Page 39
1. B
2. C
3. C
4. A
5. C

Page 40
1. C
2. D
3. B
4. C
5. D

Page 42
1. D
2. C
3. B
4. A

Page 43
1. ,
2. :
3. "
4. !
5. ,

Page 44
1. C
2. D
3. D
4. D
5. B
6. B
7. C
8. A
9. C

Page 45
1. B
2. C
3. B
4. D
5. D
6. B
7. C
8. D
9. C

Page 46
1. B
2. A
3. D
4. C
5. C
6. B

7. A
8. B
9. D
10. C

Page 47
1. B
2. D
3. B
4. C
5. B

Page 48
1. C
2. B
3. A
4. C

Page 49
1. C
2. B
3. A
4. D
5. C
6. B
7. A

Page 50
1. C
2. B
3. D
4. A
5. D
6. C

Page 51
1. D
2. B
3. C
4. A
5. C
6. D
7. A
8. B

Page 52
1. C
2. D
3. B
4. C
5. A
6. B
7. D
8. C
9. A
10. D

Page 53
1. A
2. C
3. A
4. C
5. C
6. B
7. D
8. A
9. C
10. B
11. D
12. D
13. B
14. A

Page 54
1. C
2. D
3. B
4. B
5. A
6. D
7. B

Page 55
1. C
2. D
3. A
4. B
5. D
6. B

Page 56
1. A
2. C
3. D

Page 57
1. C
2. B
3. D

Page 58
1. C
2. D
3. A
4. B

Page 59
1. C
2. D
3. A
4. C

Page 60
1. C
2. B
3. D
4. A
5. B
6. D
7. C
8. B

Page 61
1. B
2. C
3. A
4. D
5. B
6. A
7. C
8. D
9. A

Page 62
1. B
2. C
3. D
4. A
5. C

Page 63
1. B
2. C
3. D
4. C
5. B
6. B

Page 64
1. C
2. B
3. B
4. A
5. C
6. B
7. C

Page 65
1. C
2. D
3. B
4. A
5. D
6. C
7. C

Page 66
1. C
2. B
3. A
4. D
5. C
6. D
7. A
8. A
9. C

Page 67
1. C
2. C
3. B
4. A
5. D
6. C
7. B
8. B

Page 68
1. C
2. A
3. D
4. B
5. C
6. D
7. A
8. B

Page 69
1. C
2. A
3. D
4. A
5. C
6. B

Page 70
1. C
2. A
3. B
4. A
5. D
6. C
7. B
8. A
9. C
10. C
11. A
12. B
13. D
14. A
15. C

16. B
17. C
18. D

Page 71
1. C
2. D
3. C
4. C
5. A
6. B

Page 72
1. C
2. B
3. C

Page 73
1. C
2. A
3. D
4. B
5. D
6. C

Page 74
1. D
2. B
3. A
4. C

Page 75
1. D
2. B
3. C
4. B

Page 76
1. C
2. D
3. A
4. B
5. C
6. D

Page 77
1. D
2. B
3. C
4. A
5. A

Page 78
1. D
2. C
3. D
4. B
5. D

Page 79
1. C
2. D
3. A
4. B

Page 80
1. ③
2. ②
3. ③
4. ①
5. ④

Page 81
1. D
2. A
3. C
4. D
5. B
6. C

Page 82
1. c
2. d
3. c
4. a
5. b

Page 83
1. b
2. a
3. d
4. c
5. d

Page 84
1. c
2. a
3. b
4. c
5. a

Page 85
1. A
2. C
3. B
4. C
5. B

Page 86
1. D
2. C
3. A
4. B
5. D

Page 87
1. C
2. D
3. B
4. C
5. D
6. B

Page 88
1. C
2. B
3. D
4. C
5. A

Page 89
1. C
2. C
3. D
4. A
5. B
6. C

Page 90
1. B
2. C
3. D
4. A
5. C
6. A
7. D

Page 91
1. C
2. C
3. D
4. A

Page 92
1. D
2. B
3. C
4. A
5. D